Modern Leadership Lessons From the World's Greatest

Discover Timeless Qualities of 8 Extraordinary Leaders and How to Develop These Game-Changing Skills in Yourself

Paul A. Wyatt

Table of Contents

Introduction

How would you define a great leader? Are they strong? Are they caring? Are they someone you aspire to be like? Are they a person you respect, or are they a person you fear? Is a great leader born, or are they made?

It's difficult to describe a great leader. There have been leaders that many would describe as being great, but some would describe as being a tyrant. Some leaders have left a great legacy behind them, but does that make them a great leader? Other leaders have done great deeds in their time, but does a great deed, in turn, make the leader a great one?

It's simple enough to define greatness, but how do you define a great leader?

Great leaders are scattered throughout history, and we have spent years watching them and learning from them. You may believe that greatness is something you are born with, but it is actually something that you can learn. Great leaders throughout history have seen themselves as teachers, but only to those who are willing to learn.

If you are seeking the secret to being a great leader, you must first ask yourself if you are ready to learn what it means to be great.

What is the difference between a leader and a great leader? A leader is someone that others must follow because they have to, but a great leader is someone that others follow because they want to. Inspiring someone to have greatness is the reason why you would choose to follow someone rather than being forced to follow someone for one reason or another.

Great leadership has the potential to achieve extraordinary things. It excites people and demands their loyalty. Leadership is the highest of callings, but it is also the hardest calling you can take. Measuring yourself up against leaders throughout history and great people who have led the world in the past can be daunting, but that is where this book comes in handy.

If your actions inspire others to learn more, do more, dream more, and become more, you are a leader; but are you a great leader? The easiest way to differentiate a good leader from a great leader is through their qualities. You can be a good leader and inspire others to follow you, but if you are a great leader, you inspire others to also become leaders.

Great leaders are:

- Authentic
- Decisive
- Brave
- Character-driven
- Humble
- Engaging
- Goal-oriented
- A Listener
- Inspiring
- Wise
- Knowledgeable

- Optimistic
- Noble
- Motivating
- Optimistic
- Reliable
- Trustworthy
- Supportive
- A Visionary

You'll find that all of these qualities have been related to greatness and being a great leader. However, the truly great people we have seen throughout history that have led millions into a new world did not have all of these qualities, yet they were still great.

It's been hard for modern entrepreneurs and aspiring leaders to find the secret to true greatness. That's why I decided to write this book. Being a leader is hard, and it's even harder to know what makes you a leader. What makes people want to follow you? What qualities do people need to see in you in order to choose to follow your lead?

Abraham Lincoln was a man who lived a humble life, but he strived for greatness. He reached out and grabbed what everyone around him said that he couldn't have.

Mahatma Gandhi came from the smallest and most insignificant of backgrounds, but he knew that he was meant for more, so he worked hard in order to achieve it.

Mother Teresa wanted to live a simple life, but a life filled with travel and a sense for greatness called to her. How could she refuse it?

Bill Gates had a privileged childhood, coming from a wealthy background and going to the best schools that would take him, but he knew that his ancestry alone would not carry him through life. He worked hard and strived for something better than what his genetics gave him.

The world told Nelson Mandela that he was meant for one thing, to walk in the shadow of others who forced their leadership on him. Nelson Mandela did not agree with this for he knew there was a better way to lead the world, even if he did not yet know that he would be that world's leader.

Stephen Hawking was told by many that he would not live to be over 20, but he went on to marry the love of his life at the age of 26 and do incredible and great things until his eventual death at the age of 76.

These are just some of the greatest leaders this world has ever seen. They left their mark on the world and left a history of teachings behind for us to learn from. What do all of these leaders have in common? Was it their qualities that inspired those around them to follow them? It might have been, but then again, they were all completely different leaders. So what is it that connects them all?

All of these leaders have one thing in common. They strived for more, which means they strived for greatness. The world dealt them their hand, and they said they wanted more. They each had their own qualities, and they each led their followers in different ways, but they each knew they were destined for greatness.

You, too, can reach that greatness if you are willing to strive for it. In this book, you will find the qualities that many great leaders share, learn how to find and develop those qualities in yourself, and discover the lessons that leaders throughout history have been eager to teach those who are willing to learn.

1

Unlocking the Secrets of Greatness

Defining Leadership and a Great Leader

"Don't follow the crowd, let the crowd follow you."

- Margaret Thatcher

When we think of a leader, we will often think of the people in charge. These may be high-ranking people such as politicians, the president, CEOs of companies, and even your boss. However, being in this high-ranking position is not what makes someone a leader.

Leadership isn't about the position you hold or the title you have. You may have worked for years to get into a position of seniority, or you might have won a popular vote in order to gain that position, but that does not mean you have the qualities and skills needed to lead a team.

What makes a good leader? It is about more than just titles and positions. What is it that makes someone not just a leader but a great one? Greatness and leadership come

1

from more than just experience. They also require certain qualities within a person.

Leadership is described as a process by which one person encourages and motivates others to participate in the completion of a specific job. This definition falls short of what actually defines the specific paths taken by many individuals who are now regarded as the world's most outstanding leaders. All of the great leaders of the past had something special about them. They are all united by their greatness. The special qualities they used to define themselves are what enabled them to lead people towards new ideas, philosophies, and better futures.

Eight Qualities That Lead to Greatness

"The greatest leader is not necessarily the one who does the greatest things. He is the one that gets the people to do the greatest things."

- Ronald Reagan

Every quality of a great leader is meant to inspire others into greatness as well. Confidence and knowledge can carry you to great places, but the way you hold yourself up must come second to the way you hold up others. People will only follow those who know how to lead.

- Optimism
  Optimism, enthusiasm, and passion are the things that a great leader needs. Being optimistic about your current project or situation is the first step toward ensuring that your followers are just as enthused by the job as you are. Great leaders under-

2

stand that the energy they put into their current project or situation will be met by their followers. If you are hopeful, helpful, and enthusiastic about the job, your followers will be too.

You can't just pretend to be optimistic in order to save face. It's easy to spot fake optimism. You have to show true passion in your work. Allow your followers to see your enthusiasm, and your optimism will soon become contagious.

Someone who worked with Elon Musk on the SpaceX project during its early stages said that the thing that truly drove the success of the project was the enthusiasm that Elon Musk had for space travel.

- Decisiveness
A great leader does not simply take on the task of making decisions because it is their duty as a leader, but rather they welcome the risk of decision making. With greatness comes the responsibility to hold oneself accountable first and foremost if a bad decision is made. A great leader does not stress day and night, unable to make a decision. A great leader is a decisive one.

- Integrity
A great leader will exhibit integrity at all times. Integrity entails giving credit where credit is due, putting the safety and quality of their followers and their service before anything else, acknowledging and making up for mistakes, and doing what's right even if that isn't the best thing for the current project or situation. A leader with no integrity is a leader who does not have the trust of their followers.

- Humility
  A great leader does not think they are without fault or that they simply cannot make a mistake. No one is perfect, and if you try to place yourself on a pedestal above your followers, you will lose their loyalty quickly.

  Humility is the driving force of any great leader. Being able to admit to your faults and show that you are not above those that follow you wins you not only true loyalty from your followers but also their hard work and confidence.

  Accepting your failures with grace makes you a good leader, and striving to beat every failure and better yourself is what makes you a great leader.

- Authenticity
  To be authentic, no part of you can be fake. Your personality, the passion you have for your job, the way you treat people, and your loyalty all have to be genuine. People look for authenticity when they're looking for great leaders. They want to know that every part of you is true and that they aren't seeing a mask you put on in order to be what they want you to be.

  You can't pretend to be a great leader; you either are, or you aren't.

- Loyalty
  The difference between a leader and a great leader is knowing that true loyalty is reciprocal. You cannot expect your followers to be loyal to you if you do not show them loyalty in return. A great leader knows that they are in a position of service to their

4

followers, not the other way around. If your followers know that you are just as loyal to them as they are to you, they will be more likely to show you that loyalty at the times when it matters the most.

- Charisma
  Put simply, people are more likely to follow someone that they like. Charisma is a great leader's most important quality. The greatest leaders throughout time were friendly, well-spoken, approachable, and showed sincerity to others. Being a people person can make sure that your followers can relate to you, and that is how you know that you have the makings of a great leader.

- Empowerment
  In order to be a great leader, you need to have faith in your abilities to empower your followers. Empowering them entails giving them the tools they need to be confident in themselves and their abilities to do their jobs well. When you empower your followers, you can be sure that they will make decisions that are in the best interest of the current project or situation. Being an empowering leader means having trust in your followers, having confidence in their abilities, training them, and helping them develop all the skills they need.

In order to be a great leader, you need to have every single one of these eight qualities. You can't pick and choose which ones suit you best. Only these eight qualities can lead you to greatness. Without these qualities, you will be unable to recognize your full potential as a leader, and as a result, your followers will never be able to grow and realize their potential either.

Your Greatest Qualities as a Leader

"Do not follow where the path may lead. Go instead where there is no path and leave a trail."

- Ralph Waldo Emerson

What is greatness? Greatness is being able to distinguish yourself from others. When you set yourself apart from the crowd, you are truly eminent in your field. A combination of both qualities and actions is required to make someone truly great. You might think of yourself as a great leader or someone who is destined for greatness. The only question you need to ask yourself is this: Are you a leader, or are you a follower?

Becoming a great leader is not just about your qualities as a leader but rather about your greatness. You do not have to be a leader to be great. Both followers and leaders can be great. So, your quest is not to be a great leader but to achieve greatness.

Knowing what qualities you have and what your best qualities are is the first step to greatness. Here you'll find a short exercise you can use to decide which of your qualities are your best and how you can develop them or build new qualities.

Step One: Search for Feedback

Your first task is to collect feedback from multiple people, both inside your life and outside. Feedback from others helps you get a clearer picture, as it is difficult for us to be honest with ourselves. Other people will be more honest and see you as you truly are. Their feedback is what you need to find your qualities.

Your feedback needs to come from a large variety of sources. These can be your friends, family, colleagues from your present and past, your teachers, and so on. This will help you develop a much richer and broader understanding of yourself and your qualities.

You are searching for the best qualities that others see in you, so ask this question exactly. What are the best qualities that others think of when they think of you? It's best to ask them this question over email or text. People are more likely to be honest with you through an email than in person, where they may feel pressured to say something nice. You can ask for honesty and take their feedback wholeheartedly.

Step Two: Recognize Your Patterns

Now that you have received your feedback, search for patterns in that feedback. Examining the common themes that everyone who you asked brought up will help you further hone in on what your best qualities are. While searching for patterns in the feedback, try and attach them to your own memories.

For example, if someone remembers how kind you are, ask them for at least three examples. If they are able to give you multiple examples, that means you are often kind, which makes it more of a habit than something you have done once or twice. If another mentions your kindness, ask them for more examples. Connecting qualities that multiple people assign to you to certain memories is a good step to take and will help you with the next step in this process.

Sometimes we do not recognize a quality that we have. If you give out kindness often enough, it becomes more of an unconscious behavior, and you hardly notice it anymore. Your best qualities will seem like second nature to you and ones that you can use on your journey to greatness.

Once you find your patterns and recognize those qualities, mark them down in a chart from your best qualities to your least. This portion of the exercise can help you see yourself more clearly. It serves to both integrate the feedback you've received as well as build a larger picture of yourself and your capabilities.

Step Three: Compose a Portrait of Yourself

Now you can use the feedback you've received to write a description of yourself. This description needs to summarize the accumulated information you've received into one quick description. This description needs to blend the patterns you found in the information with your own experiences and memories of those patterns into a complement of who you are at your best self.

This description is your portrait, but it should not be used as a complete cognitive and physiological profile. It is an insightful image that you can use to remind yourself of your best qualities and use as a guide towards bettering your future self.

This portrait you compose should start with the phrase, "When I am at my best, I..." Write two to four paragraphs to fill in that sentence. For example, "When I am at my best, I help others selflessly, not expecting anything in return. I am strong when I need to be, and I am always ready to take on a challenge. I trust those around me and am loyal to those who have earned it." This is a short example, and yours should be longer, putting together all of the best qualities that you found through your feedback.

Take your time to compose this portrait. Do not rush it. Use careful consideration when putting all of this information together.

Step Four: Redesign Yourself

Once you have pinpointed your best qualities, you can choose to develop them further or build on other qualities that you want to have but don't. You can also try to build your world around your best qualities in order to utilize them. Pick a job that uses the most of you and your qualities. You can even choose hobbies that build on those qualities in your spare time.

Building on your best qualities and working to develop others is the best way to create yourself the way you want to. You know the qualities that are seen in most of the greatest leaders, and you now know if you possess those qualities or not.

This exercise helps you find your strengths so that you can build on them. Knowing your strengths offers you a chance to build your life around them rather than take on a job or activity that plays against what you are strong at. In other words, if you are good at leading but horrible at numbers, you can lead a business, but you'll need to get a finance partner to help you with the numbers.

There are a few things you need to keep in mind after completing this exercise:

- Accept your weaknesses

  By finding your best qualities, you'll also be highlighting your weaknesses. Sometimes this can be a little disheartening for those who weren't aware of what their worst qualities or their weaknesses are.

  It's okay to have weaknesses, and accepting them is your first step to bettering yourself. If you shy away from your weaknesses, you can't turn them into your strengths. You can be changed, and not everything is set in stone, so do not see them as weaknesses because they do not have to stay that way.

- Differentiate your strengths from your talents

  People often confuse their strengths with their talents. There are your best qualities, and then there are things that you are simply good at. They are very different things. Strengths are seen as traits that can be developed and learned through effort, but talents are seen as natural qualities that people inherit through genetics. Sometimes it's difficult to tell the difference between the two, so you have to be honest with yourself.

  Remember that strengths and talents can blur together sometimes. Juggling is learned as a trained strength but is made easier if you have a natural genetic talent for balance and coordination. Good social skills develop as a strength through conscious effort, but that development gets a kick start if genetics have given you a pleasing appearance that draws people towards you. Think about what innate talents you may have and try to use them to the fullest by putting in the time to turn them into proper strengths.

2

Abraham Lincoln - The Freer of Slaves and the Symbol of Liberty

"That some achieve great success, is proof to all that others can achieve it as well."

- Abraham Lincoln

A braham Lincoln was the 16th President of the United States, serving in his role as a leader of the nation from 1861 to 1865. His presidency lasted a little more than four years, and in that short amount of time, he became a hero, a symbol, and is now renowned as one of the greatest presidents in history in terms of his character and political acumen.

Abraham Lincoln was not only a great man, a great president, and a great symbol for mankind; he was also a great leader.

A Nation Divided

Abraham Lincoln had many achievements throughout his life. One of his most notable achievements was during his time as President of the United States, when he helped the nation triumph through its greatest challenge: the Civil War.

Lincoln came from humble beginnings. He was born in 1809 as the second child to Thomas Lincoln and Nancy Hanks Lincoln. He was raised in a log cabin before their family migrated to the west. His parents were simple people who lived simple lives, never knowing that Abraham was destined for greatness.

At the time of Lincoln's presidency, the nation was divided into two factions: the northern states and the southern states. Their war was waged over the right to own slaves. Most of the southern states in the U.S. allowed their citizens to legally own slaves. However, the northern states where slaves were emancipated and allowed to live free lives were known as free states at the time. Abraham Lincoln was part of the free states, and he believed in the rights of all mankind, with one of those rights being the right to freedom and liberty.

Abraham Lincoln supported the Union in their opposition to slavery. The southern states supported slavery, and when Lincoln won the presidential election in 1860, they were displeased. One of Lincoln's promises as president was the emancipation of all slaves. His election caused the states to divide.

South Carolina was the first state to secede from the Union on December 20, 1860, as they wanted to distance themselves from the Union before Abraham Lincoln could be sworn in as president. Soon other southern states followed South Carolina, and they would form The Confederate States of America. Jefferson Davis was elected their president, effectively splitting the United States into two nations.

The splitting of the United States would not be the end of it. Abraham Lincoln was elected president in March, and in April, before he even had the chance to settle into the White House, Fort Sumter in North Carolina was attacked by Confederate forces. This marked the beginning of the Civil War.

Abraham Lincoln had to take up the role of president during one of the United States' most difficult times, and because of this, many of the decisions he made while in office have had a huge impact on our lives today. Every one of the choices that Lincoln made shaped the nation and built the lives of many who now live in the United States. It is for this reason he is considered a great leader, and his achievements as a leader are his legacy.

His Presidency

When many think of the election of Abraham Lincoln, they regard it as being the reason behind the nation being divided and the start of the Civil War. This is not accurate. Before his presidency began in 1860, the nation was already divided. The south and the north had different opinions on almost everything, from racial rights and slavery to women's rights. Their split opinions on slavery eventually led to the rift. Since the northern states were made free for all slaves, it encouraged many of the slaves from southern states to escape to the north in order to find their freedom. It's true that Abraham Lincoln's inauguration only furthered that divide, but he took it in stride.

Becoming President of the United States is considered one of his great achievements since it was done in such a difficult time. Not many could have been strong enough to lead a divided nation through a war. It is not his greatest achievement by far, but it is worthy of being noted.

Winning a Second Term

When Lincoln's first term as president was up, he fought for his reelection. Winning the presidential election for the second time was one of his greatest achievements, as he required the support of voters in order to keep fighting the war. His term ended before the Civil War. If someone else had been voted into the presidency during this time, the outcome could have been completely different. Lincoln needed to win the war, and he had enough supporters to make this happen.

He was voted into his second term as President of the United States because many believed in his leadership, and many others voted for him because of the emancipation proclamation.

Preserving the Union

Abraham Lincoln worked hard toward preserving part of the Union. Many southern states left the Union, forming their own Confederate States. The secession of 13 states from the Union was a huge blow to the Country, but Lincoln did his best to keep the damage to a minimum.

During the Civil War, the Lincoln administration did its job by preventing a few states from leaving with the 13 southern states. Lincoln did this by targeting the border states. The main reason for the secession was that citizens wanted to keep their right to own slaves. Lincoln realized this and allowed many border states who still had slavery to retain their slaves in order to stop them from leaving.

This was seen by many as a poor decision and far from the morals that Lincoln stood for, but as the president, he needed to preserve as much of the Union as he could. The border states stayed with the Union and were eventually made to release their slaves when Lincoln released the emancipation proclamation.

The Emancipation Proclamation

This is high up on the list of Abraham Lincoln's achievements and is one of his greatest. The Emancipation Proclamation was a step towards creating rights for slaves and freeing them. It was not a direct victory for this goal, but it was a huge step towards it.

This was not Abraham Lincoln's accomplishment, but he was the one who signed it into law, and he did so just in time to help turn the war around. The Emancipation Proclamation did not set all slaves free the moment it was issued. The country was still deep in war when it was first issued into law in 1863. Instead, the proclamation gave African Americans the right to serve in both the Navy and the Army of the Union.

This turned the tide of the war. The Union was badly outnumbered, and they were in desperate need of troops. With the issuing of the proclamation, more than 200,000 African Americans joined the armed forces and were happy to finally have the right to serve their country. Lincoln gave them the right to fight for their own freedom, and they jumped at the opportunity.

The Emancipation Proclamation did also state that the slaves were to be freed; however, this did not apply to the Confederate States or any of the border states. The states that it did apply to were already slave-free at the time, but it put the first foot forward towards eventually freeing all slaves and giving them rights.

Winning the Civil War

Winning the Civil War is one of Lincoln's greatest achievements, if not his greatest, but it is not the fact that he helped the Union states win the war that he should be remembered for. It is his actions and attitude after winning the war that many should think of when they think of this achievement. Abraham Lincoln had helped the Union states fight day and night while losing many soldiers, celebrating the smallest of victories, and regretting every defeat. When he finally fought the last battle and won the whole war, he was not a cruel dictator but a humble victor.

Instead of dealing out harsh punishment, he set out straight away to send relief efforts to the losing states. He did not want to hold his victory over their heads and make them pay for their decision to leave the Union. Instead, he wanted to help them grow and rise along with the Union. He wanted to rebuild the country as a whole so that all the states could rise together and once again be great.

It is unfortunate that Lincoln could not fully see the country that he wanted to build. His relief efforts were cut short quickly due to his assassination. If it hadn't been for John Wilkes Booth's bullet, the south would likely have recovered from the war and rejoined the country a lot sooner. However, after Lincoln's death the efforts were brought to a halt, and another smaller war started again. This time, the north overpowered the south and made sure they paid for their actions.

Ending Slavery

Abraham Lincoln might not have been the direct accomplisher of this feat, and he might not have been around to see it finally come into the light, but he is still seen as the hand that guided others towards this decision.

The Emancipation Proclamation, signed into law by Lincoln, did not end up freeing any slaves, even though it stated that was its intention. However, it did wind up giving slaves the right to join the armed forces, and it forced many African Americans and Whites to work together in close quarters. It was the first step that eventually led to the 13th Amendment.

After the war and before his death, Lincoln continued to support the legislation that would effectively lead to the freedom of slaves. He supported the 13th Amendment during his lifetime, and it would eventually be the thing to end slavery.

This is seen as Abraham Lincoln's greatest achievement, even though he was not alive to see it happen. His efforts to give slaves rights and create a free country for all would eventually shape the world we live in today.

From Humble Beginnings to Great Endings

"Be sure you put your feet in the right place, then stand firm."

- Abraham Lincoln

It has been more than 150 years since the assassination of Abraham Lincoln, which was a tragic event that brought his great life to a halt. Still, he is an inspiration to us all, and his ideals continue to be something that people looking for greatness strive for. His words of wisdom and great deeds are life lessons for us all.

To truly appreciate his greatness, you must understand the steps he took along his journey through life.

The Humblest Beginning

When we see someone who has achieved greatness in their lives, it's often hard to imagine them coming from a small and humble background. In fact, some people believe that if you are not born into greatness, then you can't achieve it. This couldn't be further from the truth. Many people who have achieved greatness in their lives, including some of history's greatest leaders, come from the most humble beginnings.

Abraham Lincoln is widely known as a great leader and one of the greatest presidents America has ever had, but not many know he was a simple farm boy. Lincoln's parents, Thomas and Nancy Hanks Lincoln, were simple people that lived simple lives. Abraham was born on Sinking Springs Farm in a one-room log cabin.

Thomas was a carpenter and farmer by trade, and by the time Abraham was born, his father already controlled or owned a small number of farms in the area. However, Abraham would not live his life here due to his father losing most of his farmland in property deed disputes. The family would eventually pack up and travel to Indiana for a new beginning only two years after Abraham was born.

The Lincoln family moved from Kentucky, a state that allowed the owning of slaves, to Indiana, which was considered 'free' territory. The state did not allow its residents to own slaves. The fact that Abraham moved to a free state with his family instead of staying in Kentucky likely influenced the decisions he would make later in life. Abraham Lincoln's stance on slavery can possibly be tracked to this very decision his family made to move to Indiana.

Abraham was raised in Hurricane Township, where his father worked hard as a farmer, carpenter, and cabinet maker to support his family. Thomas Lincoln eventually recouped the money he lost in Kentucky and managed to buy up at least 80 acres of land, starting up the Little Pigeon Creek community.

Abraham would soon join his father in working on the farm, as many young boys did back then, once they reached the age where they could start working. However, when Abraham was only nine years old, he lost his mother to milk sickness. His 11-year-old sister would then take up the duties of the woman in the house and become his chief caretaker until his father remarried a woman who had three children of her own. The loss of his mother was hard for Abraham, but he soon grew close to his step-mother and even called her mother.

It is important for anyone who wants to understand Abraham Lincoln's journey to greatness to know that he came from very small beginnings. He was just a farm boy, working hard on his father's farm and enduring hardships like losing his mother at the age of 9 and having to grow accustomed to a new, larger family.

The Love of Learning

Abraham Lincoln started out as a humble farm boy, and he worked hard to help his father around the farm, but he always preferred reading and writing to all of that farm work. A small but important detail many tend to miss about Abraham Lincoln is that he was largely self-educated.

Abraham preferred to read and write, but at the time, many around him saw this as pure laziness and an excuse to avoid doing work. Even with this backward thinking on education, Abraham continued working towards bettering his education. Although he was mostly self-taught, he would learn from time to time from teachers who passed through the town. Abraham would have only 12 months of formal education while growing up.

During his childhood, Abraham would read titles like *The Pilgrim's Progress*, the Bible, *Aesop's Fables*, and Benjamin Franklin and George Washington's biographies.

Along with his education, Abraham also exercised his physical strength. He continued to do farm work along with a few odd jobs around the town, and he even earned himself a reputation for his strength by besting the leader of a group of bullies, Clary's Grove boys, in a fight. He gave all of his earnings to his father in order to help with the family. The family would eventually move again when Abraham was 21 years old. He accompanied them to their new home in Macon County, Ill. However, when the family prepared to move again the next year, Abraham made the decision to go out on his own.

Abraham was a family man and a hard worker, but he valued his education and learning above everything else. He continued to learn and work as he lived in the town of New Salem on his own for the next six years. The many jobs he had included a soldier, boatman, rail splitter, surveyor, and postmaster. He even owned and operated his own general store. He continued to further his education, and in 1834, he ran for representative to the Illinois General Assembly and was elected. In the next two years, he worked to earn his license to practice law.

Life, Love, Hardships, and Greatness

Abraham's work was not done after he earned his license to practice law. It took hard work and dedication for him to rise this high up without a formal education, but he could not stop there. Abraham Lincoln was determined to reach greatness in his life in more than one way.

He moved to Springfield, Ill., and became a junior partner of John Todd Stuart's law firm. It was through Stuart that he met the daughter of a Kentucky slave owner, Mary Todd, and three years later, they would be wed. He went on to work towards greatness while growing a family with his new wife, welcoming their first child, Robert Todd Lincoln, into the world the same year that Abraham Lincoln established his very own law office.

Abraham won a seat in the U.S. Congress soon after the birth of his second son. This was his first step into the world of politics and his eventual presidency. Abraham and his family moved to Washington D.C. because of his new position in Congress, but his wife would later take the children back to Springfield so Abraham could focus on his work. Abraham disagreed with this decision, but he continued to work, and a few years later, he would be responsible for introducing the bill that would eventually abolish slavery within Washington D.C.

Only a year later, in February, Abraham would be given the news of the death of his youngest son, Edward, who was barely four years old. It is believed that he died of tuberculosis. In December of the same year, his wife gave birth to a third son, William, and two years later, another son, Thomas. Abraham's family was growing steadily, as were his ambitions.

His Legacy

It's enough for a good man to leave behind a life well-lived, but it is expected of a great man to leave behind a legacy. That is what Abraham Lincoln has done. He was the greatest politician and the greatest president that the United States ever had. He led the nation through its most trying time, and he showed his greatness to all who watched.

He has left behind not only stories but legends. His greatest contributions during his lifetime were to preserve the Union, effectively stopping the country from falling apart throughout the war between the states. His abolishment of slavery and his championship skills in democracy are also his great achievements.

His legacy still shapes the world we live in today. The way he led the country and the influence he had during the Civil War and the divided nation still move and dictate the things we do today. That is the legacy of a great man and a great leader.

Lessons of Life and Leadership from Abraham Lincoln

"The best way to destroy an enemy is to make him a friend."

- Abraham Lincoln

Abraham Lincoln is considered an icon of wisdom, resolve, compassion, and patience. He has shown passion for his goals, determination in reaching those goals, courage when faced with threats and danger, humility in losing, and mercy in winning.

Along with his legacy, Abraham has left behind lessons for those striving for greatness like him. These lessons are not only for greatness as a leader, but also for greatness in life.

Compassion

The compassion that Abraham Lincoln showed was not limited to his followers or his friends, but also extended to his enemies. He knew that there was suffering on both sides of the war and that both the northern and the southern states were losing lives. He knew that ending the war would not only mean relief for him and his friends, but relief for his enemies as well. After all, he believed that making his enemies his friends would be the best way to destroy them.

Mercy

When the war was won and the southern states surrendered to the northern states, Abraham did not relish in his victory. He did not celebrate, he did not think to punish his enemies, and he did not enjoy his victory as many others would have if they won a war. Instead, Abraham's thoughts were on rebuilding the nation as a whole, and this meant helping his enemies.

Abraham did not deal out harsh punishments for the southern states leaving the Union, striking out on their own, and waging war against the northern states. Any thoughts of punishment did not even occur to him. He did not see them as his enemies. He saw them as his people, and they needed his help.

Abraham showed mercy where some would have not, and this is what set him apart.

Humility

Showing mercy in victory is only one half of the puzzle; showing humility in defeat as well as victory is what you need to complete the puzzle. Abraham knew that his position as president did not put him above others. He was humble and saw all others as his equals.

Showing such humility towards your followers and seeing them as your equals is the best way to gain their respect. Abraham understood this.

Compromise

One of Abraham Lincoln's greatest qualities was his ability to compromise. When the first southern states left the Union, and he saw many others following in their footsteps, he knew he had to do something to preserve as much of the Union as possible. He did this by convincing the border states to remain with the Union. He struck up a deal through compromise.

Abraham did not believe in slavery, and one of his main goals was to abolish it completely, but he put aside that goal for a moment and focused on the bigger picture. He compromised with the border states, allowing them to keep their slaves in order for them to remain with the Union.

Compromise is an essential skill for any great leader to have.

Strive for More

Abraham did not know for certain if he was meant for greatness. He was born into a humble home and lived a humble life. There was nothing in his life that meant he was destined for more, but that did not stop him from striving for it.

Abraham pushed himself beyond his limits and conquered every challenge he set for himself. He did not see obstacles in his way. He saw opportunities. If you can take anything away from Abraham Lincoln's life, it is that not everyone is born into greatness and not everyone is destined for it, but those that want it can strive for it.

3

Mahatma Gandhi - The Man With a Global Legacy

"A man is but the product of his thoughts. What he thinks, he becomes."

\- Mahatma Gandhi

Mahatma Gandhi is one of history's most revered and significant freedom fighters. He was an anti-war activist and the man who left behind a legacy for the world to follow. He is regarded all around the world for his non-violent movement. He was a pacifist and tried to show others that violence was not the answer to the world's problems. He believed in the rights of others and strived to see his beliefs come to fruition. He was the father of a nation and the leader of a new world.

The Father of the Nation

Mahatma Gandhi was born in 1869 in India, back when it was still part of the British Empire. His activism as an Indian immigrant started in the early 1900s in the years following World War I. He began in South Africa as he became the leading figure in the struggle for India's independence from Great Britain.

He was labeled the Father of the Nation in India, and he was known as "the great-souled one." Gandhi's pursuit for freedom and the rights of his people led him to be imprisoned many times and undertake several hunger strikes, all in the name of his cause. He never stood down, and he never gave up on his beliefs.

It all started in South Africa after Mahatma Gandhi had finished his schooling and earned the right to practice law. He completed his law studies in London and got a call to the bar in 1891. He took up a position as a lawyer for an Indian businessman and trader stationed in Johannesburg, South Africa. Mahatma Gandhi loved his home in India, but since he was unable to establish a law practice that could thrive in his home country, he moved to South Africa, where he was offered the best opportunities for him to practice law.

He ended up spending over two decades in South Africa, shaping its ideals with his beliefs and changing its ways through his nonviolent actions. Gandhi could never fully realize his potential in the past. He was always shy, softly spoken, and did not enjoy speaking in front of crowds. This is one of the reasons why he was unable to stay in London, where he learned and practiced law. He was not fit for it. However, during his stay in South Africa, he truly came out of his shell and refined his beliefs, social views, political ideas, and thoughts on the environment.

One of Gandhi's main motivators during his stay in South Africa was the way he was treated. He received the harshest of discriminations on an almost daily basis due to the color of his skin. Race was a common issue in South Africa at the time.

Gandhi did not believe in violence, but he believed in standing up for what he thought was right; this also meant standing against what he believed to be wrong. He did so by refusing to conform to the laws of the country that discriminated against him. He would protest on buses and trains. One such protest ended up with him being thrown off a train for refusing to give up his seat to a white woman. He also received beatings on multiple occasions for his individual protests. In one instance, he was ordered to remove his turban by a judge, but he refused.

It was clear to Gandhi that his people were being treated poorly, and he saw it as his duty to do something about it. So shortly after his contract of employment had expired, he made the decision to stay in South Africa. At first, his goal was to protest the newly passed law that would have infringed the voting rights of all Indians living in South Africa. He worked hard, but the bill would be passed in 1896 despite his efforts. His journey had only just begun.

During his stay in South Africa, Gandhi worked to unite Indians from all walks of life and work. He helped bring many individuals together and forced the world to change how they perceived people of color.

Gandhi did more than just work towards the fair treatment of Indians living in South Africa. When his work was done there, he also returned home to India and continued to work towards the country's freedom. He became a political and spiritual leader, and many followed him into his nonviolent, non-cooperative campaigns. He brought to light how important it was that India receive economic independence.

During his efforts to free India as a nation, he also worked hard to bring the internally divided nation back together. The country of India was shared between Hindus and Muslims. Gandhi followed the Hindu belief, but he wanted both Hindus and Muslims to live in peace together.

He worked for both freedom and peace, but in the end, he would only be granted one of these things. After all of his efforts, negotiations between Britain, the Muslim League, and the Congress Party led to an agreement and India was granted its independence from Britain in 1947. This was sadly after Gandhi had announced his retirement from politics in 1934 and resigned from the Congress Party. He did so in order to concentrate more on his efforts in the more rural communities. He realized his dream of a free India, but not his dream of a united India, as the country was split into two domains: Pakistan and India. Gandhi opposed this at first, but he eventually agreed to it in the hopes that Muslims and Hindus could finally achieve some form of peace after they had their independence.

Still, Gandhi had lived long enough to see his goal come to life. The ideals and dreams that he had worked towards his whole life had finally come to be. His nonviolent ways and his strong mentality would prove triumphant over those who thought his efforts to be done in vain.

Gandhi was shot and killed in 1948. He left behind a legacy that would live on forever, and the next day around 1 million people followed the procession. They carried Gandhi's body through the streets of Delhi to the banks of the holy Jumna River, where he was cremated.

Many followed him in life, and many more followed him in death, making him one of the world's greatest leaders.

A Life Without Violence

Mahatma Gandhi's greatest achievement in his life is considered to be his contributions to India's independence from Britain through nonviolent and non-cooperative protests. He was an anti-war activist and the father of a nation, but he had many other achievements throughout his lifetime. These include achievements that some might see as small or insignificant and achievements that are seen as large and monumental. All of these achievements form the life that Mahatma Gandhi lived and the legacy that he left behind.

The Passive Resistance Campaign

One of Gandhi's many accomplishments was the birth of passive resistance. In 1906, the Transvaal government passed an ordinance that required the registration of the Indian population. The Asiatic Law Amendment Ordinance was signed into law, and it was both discriminatory and humiliating towards any Indians living in the Transvaal. The law forced Indians to register with the 'registrar of Asiatics,' provide fingerprints, submit to a physical examination, and carry around a registration certificate with them at all times. Failure to do so would result in a fine, imprisonment, or deportation. It was known as the 'Black Act.'

This started an eight-year-long campaign of civil disobedience. This Act did not only affect the Indians; some Chinese and Africans were also affected. Thousands stood against this Act. A delegation of Indians sailed to London and met with the Secretary of State, who was Lord Elgin at the time. He would go on to publicly renounce the Black Act, but in private, all he did was advocate for a few superficial revisions to the Act.

When the day came for the certificate offices to open in 1907, resistors launched an effort to camp outside the offices and dissuade any passing Indians from going inside and registering. They gathered support for their non-cooperation movement, and it came to be known as the 'Passive Resistance Campaign,' but Gandhi gave it the term 'Satyagraha," which literally translates to 'truth-force.' This movement developed as a paradigm for any and all nonviolent struggle that advocated for active resistance to oppression. It would go on to influence the struggle for Indian independence in decades to follow.

When the registration closed, only 511 Indians out of the 13,000 in the region had actually been registered. Those who did register were shamed by the resisters. Some would even tear up the certificates afterward. In response to this, hundreds of the resisters, known as satyagrahis, were jailed, and an unfortunate few were even deported. This included several African-born Indians. Still, the passive resistance towards the Act continued.

Gandhi himself was arrested in 1908 and the jails were rapidly filling with many satyagrahis that refused to register. General J.C. Smuts was forced to negotiate better terms with the resisters. General Smuts presented them with an ultimatum. He claimed that if the Indians would agree to register voluntarily, then the Black Act would be repealed, and the prisoners would be released. Gandhi agreed to this ultimatum on behalf of the resistance, but many who followed him felt betrayed by this. He was attacked, but he stood by the agreement and registered, anyway.

After Gandhi registered, General Smuts went back on his word. He went on to introduce a bill that validated the voluntary registrations, but he did nothing about the Black Act. Gandhi then took a stand because he felt betrayed by the man whose promises he believed. He gave General Smut until the 16th of August of the year 1908 to repeal the Act and fulfill his promise. This demand was ignored.

Gandhi then led the next phase of the struggle as another ultimatum was introduced. Gandhi warned that if the Black Act was not repealed, then the registration certificates would be publicly burnt. Hundreds of satyagrahis followed Gandhi and gathered outside the Hamida Mosque on August 16. When the telegram from General Smuts arrived stating that the government could not repeal the Act, over 2,000 registration certificates were burned in a giant fire.

India's First Civil Disobedience Movement

Upon his return to India in 1915, while it was still under British rule, Mahatma Gandhi won his first battle in Champaran. Champaran was a district in the state of Bhar in India. It was a land made up mostly of farms, and since it was still under British rule, the British forced the farmers within the region to grow what are known as 'cash crops' such as indigo. The farmers in the region would be made to grow these crops instead of any food crops. The farmers would then sell their crops to only British landlords, and they were forced to sell at a low fixed price.

The region suffered from this as well as harsh taxes and extremely bad weather. Due to these living conditions, the region fell into abject poverty. When Gandhi saw this, he tried to use the same methods he had used in South Africa and organize a mass uprising by the people to protest the injustice.

This is known as the Champaran Satyagraha of 1917. It was the first of Gandhi's satyagraha movements that he led in India, and it was his first popular movement. It's considered an important rebellion historically in the freedom struggle in India.

Indigo was first commercially grown in the region starting in 1750, and it was used to make dye. Due to colonial-era laws, the farmers who were tenants on their farms were forced to grow indigo using a portion of their land as one of the conditions of their tenancy. Indigo was not usually grown since it was seen as a high-need plant, requiring a lot of water and leaving the soil infertile. In order to force the farmers to grow this crop, landowners made it a condition for providing loans and incentivized its farming by lessening the rent of the farmers that grew it.

Gandhi gathered a following and adopted the same strategy he employed in South Africa of nonviolent civil disobedience. Gandhi's arrival to the area unsettled the British, and they asked him to leave. When he refused, he was arrested. The charge was creating unrest. Gandhi's arrest led to a mass of nonviolent protests and many rallies; the police eventually had to release him.

With Gandhi's release from imprisonment, the civil disobedience movement could continue. Through the movement, Gandhi was able to successfully turn the public's frustration into an effective political tool. The public's strikes and protests against the British landlords who forced them to grow Indigo crops eventually ended with the landlords agreeing to abolish the indigo cultivation on their farms. This was possible due to the 8,000 testimonies of the farmers and those living in the area that Gandhi and his colleagues collected.

The landlords, with the guidance of the British government, signed an agreement that granted farmers more control and compensation over farming on their lands and other benefits.

With this, the first civil disobedience movement implemented by Gandhi in India was over, and Gandhi went on to reuse these same methods in several of his other movements.

The Kheda Tax Revolt

The Kheda district in Gujarat, India, was devastated by famine and floods in 1918. This led to a number of problems, including crop yields being less than a fourth of what was planted. With the district suffering from all of these natural disasters, the residents pleaded with the British government to give them some relief from the already inflated and harsh taxes. The British government refused their pleas.

Mahatma Gandhi heard of this injustice and traveled to the district to provide aid. He consulted with Vallabhbhai Patel, the future Home Minister of India. Together they initiated a campaign, and Gandhi led a nonviolent protest. The residents joined his campaign and pledged non-payment of revenue.

The British government soon received the news of this protest and responded instantly. They warned that if the farmers and residents refused to pay the revenue, their land would be confiscated and the seized property would not be returned. Even with this threat and the farmers having their property seized, they stood behind Mahatma Gandhi and Vallabhbhai Patel. The nonviolent tax revolt continued.

In the month of May in 1918, after only five months, the nonviolent protest was successful. The government agreed to suspend the tax for not only that year but for the next year as well. All property that was seized during the revolt was quickly returned to the owners, and the increased rate on tax was reduced.

The Salt March

Mahatma Gandhi led the Salt March to Dandi, one of his most famous movements. The British Salt Act, implemented in 1882, prohibited Indians from selling or collecting salt, and it imposed a heavy tax on salt as well. In 1930, Gandhi decided to put a stop to this injustice.

For 24 days, from the 12th of March to the 6th of April, Mahatma Gandhi marched from Ahmedabad to Dandi, in Gujarat, which was a 241-mile distance. Gandhi planned on producing salt from seawater once he reached Dandi, which was a common practice of the local populace before the British Salt Act was implemented. This became known as the Salt March or the Dandi March.

Thousands of Indians joined Gandhi on his march, and it sparked a large act of civil disobedience against the British salt laws. Millions of Indians were involved, and the march eventually led to the imprisonment of 80,000 Indians.

This was one of Gandhi's most famous movements, even though it never led to any concessions. The British Salt Act continued to stand, and Indians were still prohibited from selling or collecting salt. Despite this, the incident received extensive coverage by the media and helped gain recognition from the world for the legitimacy of India's claim to independence.

The Salt March would go on to influence several activists on their own movements, including Martin Luther King, Jr.

Indian Ambulance Corps

While back in South Africa, Gandhi participated in the second Boer War in a nonviolent way by helping those who were injured. Mahatma Gandhi created the Natal Indian Ambulance Corps, and it was used by the British to act as stretcher bearers during the war. Gandhi and his corps served at the Battle of Spion Kop.

When the Boer attacked Natal in 1899, leading to the siege of Ladysmith, British authorities needed to recruit the Natal Volunteer Ambulance Corps. It consisted of about 1,100 local White men, but at the same time Gandhi pressed for his Indian stretcher-bearers to be allowed to serve as well. With Gandhi's participation, the corps consisted of 300 free Indians and 800 that were indentured laborers.

During the Battle of Colenso, the Natal Volunteer Ambulance Corps helped by removing the injured soldiers from the front lines. The Indians then transported the injured to the railhead for medical care. Later at the Battle of Spion Kop, the Indians were moved to the front line in order to better help remove the injured from the battlefield.

At the end of the battle, following the relief of Ladysmith, the war moved away from Natal. The corps was disbanded, and 34 of the Indian leaders, including Gandhi, were awarded the Queen's South Africa Medal. Gandhi was also awarded the 'Kaiser-i-Hind' along with other awards.

What Leaders Can Learn From His Leadership

Through his achievements and brilliant leadership, Mahatma Gandhi not only left behind a truly astounding legacy but also many lessons for others like him wanting to build on their own leadership skills.

Persistence

If there was one thing that led to Mahatma Gandhi's success as a leader, it was his persistence. A critical part of his movements was how he was always determined to see through to the end of his goal. Nothing could stop him or dissuade him from completing the journey he was on, even if it put his own well-being at risk. He is well known for sticking out a protest even when many are standing against him, standing behind his beliefs even after being imprisoned, and continuing with a strike or a fast even when it threatens his own health.

A lesson for great leaders to follow is that persistence is key to any goal you set for yourself and others.

Inner Strength Versus Outer Strength

One of the many points that Gandhi proved during his lifetime and leadership was that strength of the mind would always beat physical strength. He did this by proving over and over again that violence would gain little results, but symbols and ideas would always gain the results he wanted.

He preferred to use his thoughts and influence over physical strength through nonviolent protests, civil disobedience, and non-cooperation. He often got the results he wanted without having to resort to violence in any way. This proves that mind over body is the preferred method for any great leader.

Be Reasonable

Gandhi didn't always get his way. He was a man who stuck to his beliefs and goals, but he was also a man who could be reasoned with. He stated that he would not allow India to be divided, that it would be done over his dead body. However, he was still able to see that for India to eventually gain independence, a divide between Hindus and Muslims was inevitable.

Sticking to your goals and standing behind your beliefs no matter what is a good quality of a leader, but to be a great leader, you must be reasonable and make compromises.

Discipline

Along with his many other qualities, Gandhi constantly showed that he was disciplined. He believed in self-discipline to strengthen and improve one's self. He believed that doing this also helped him in committing to his goals. Discipline can make you a strong leader. It can help you focus on what you really want and help you commit fully to achieving any goal you set for yourself.

Showmanship

Gandhi was more than just a great leader; he was a great showman. Most of the things that Gandhi did would not have had nearly as big an impact if it weren't for Gandhi's showmanship.

The Salt March is his most famous movement against the harsh British rule. However, the reason it was so famous is because Gandhi turned it into more than just a movement. He could have completed this journey quietly. No one had to know about it in order for him to make the march. But if no one had known about it and the media hadn't covered it, it wouldn't have made as much of an impact as it did.

Being a leader also means knowing how to capture the attention of an audience. Once you have an audience, you have people listening to your ideas. Once you have people listening to your ideas, you have followers. A great leader cannot lead without followers.

4

Nelson Mandela - A Man in Search of Freedom

"Real leaders must be ready to sacrifice all for the freedom of their people."

- Nelson Mandela

Nelson Mandela is known and loved all around the world for his commitment to peace, his great negotiation skills, and his reconciliation methods. He was the first African president in South Africa and the first democratically elected president.

Mandela's achievements were great and extensive, stretching from his years in service as president and far after his presidency ended. Nelson Mandela shaped the future of South Africa and still influences the path it takes today.

The End of an Era

"Education is the most powerful weapon which you can use to change the world."

- Nelson Mandela

Nelson Mandela, born Rolihlahla Mandela, was a well-educated man. He attended several Universities, including the University of South Africa, the University of London, and the University of Witwatersrand. However, even with his high education, Mandela lived in a time of apartheid, and the apartheid laws meant that he was discriminated against greatly. Nelson Mandela decided early on that he would be devoted to ending the apartheid laws. He started his journey by joining many racial advocacy groups in order to work towards the end of apartheid.

Nelson Mandela's greatest achievement was ending apartheid, but he made many great steps on his way there. One of his major steps toward this was the African National Congress, also known as the ANC. The ANC was a group composed of Africans who agreed that they were being treated unfairly by those who were in control of South Africa at the time.

Nelson Mandela became the president of the ANC. Along with other leaders, he fought back against unjust racial laws. Their methods varied from both nonviolent protests to violent tactics and attacks. These protests, both violent and nonviolent ones, did not sit well with the government. The protests incited an uprising among the people, and the government began to fear what could come of it.

In 1962, the government fought against the protests of the ANC's movements by jailing 165 leaders, including Nelson Mandela. Their charges were conspiring to overthrow the government. Nelson Mandela was sentenced to life in prison in 1963 for his political offenses.

The government hoped that with Nelson Mandela in prison, he would be prevented from spreading his influence and leadership skills to others. Instead, without a voice to speak with, Mandela decided to write. He wrote about his thoughts and feelings since there was no one around him to listen.

During his years in prison, Mandela underwent cruel and harsh punishments, and he even contracted tuberculosis. Mandela was also offered a deal to renounce his armed struggle for early release, but he refused this offer.

His years in prison did not put a stop to his influence on the people. The protests against the unjust rule of the nation continued. After 27 long years, Mandela got his chance to speak to president F.W. de Klerk. Mandela managed to convince the president of his cause. Mandela was released from prison in 1990, and the ban that was put on the ANC was lifted.

Along with his release from prison at the age of 72, and the ban on the ANC being lifted, Mandela also brokered a deal with President Federik William de Klerk to end apartheid.

Nelson Mandela's imprisonment was meant to serve as a warning to others who threatened the government, but instead, it served as a symbol of defiance against the apartheid laws, inciting even more protests and encouraging others to stand against the laws.

Only a year after Nelson Mandela's release from prison, South Africa held its very first open election. With an open election and the right to vote given to Africans, Nelson Mandela won the first open election in South Africa and became the first Black president in South African history.

Upon winning the election, Nelson Mandela instantly turned his sights on the apartheid. He spoke about it as a "human disaster," and spoke of how it tore the country apart and caused terrible conflict. He said that the time of healing was upon them and promised the nation that it would never again witness such oppression. It is said that 100,000 South African men, women, and children danced for joy when they saw Nelson Mandela win the election.

As president of South Africa, Mandela was able to lead the country into a new era, free of segregation, free of racial discrimination, and with fairness and equality among the races. Among all of his amazing achievements, Mandela's greatest one was winning against an unjust and unfair government.

A Long Walk to Freedom

"Resentment is like drinking poison and then hoping it will kill your enemies."

\- Nelson Mandela

The greatest achievements that he is known for are what define Nelson Mandela as a great leader and a great man, but these are not the only stories he has to tell. His life was filled with inspiration. He defined what it meant to have a dream and chase it down. His stories tell us who he was as a man and help us understand him as a leader.

The Path of Justice

Nelson Mandela, the man who changed the entire shape of the world, came from the tiny village Mvezo and was part of the Madiba clan. As he grew up, he heard the elders of his village talk about the stories of their ancestors and how they fought in the war of resistance with valor. He took these stories to heart and dreamed of making his own contribution towards the struggle for freedom.

Mandela went through his own struggles as a child. Losing his father at the age of 9 was one of his biggest, but he didn't let that stop him. In order to achieve his goal of making a difference, he knew he needed an education. He was the first member of his family to even attend school.

In 1952, Nelson Mandela and his childhood friend, Oliver Tambo, used their education to set up the first African-run law firm in South Africa. Their goal was to provide legal counsel to any Africans in South Africa who had broken the laws of apartheid. Mandela mentioned in his autobiography that his law firm was seen by the people as a place where they would not be turned away or cheated and a place where they would feel proud to be represented by men with the same skin color.

This was the first step he took on his journey toward helping his own people find their freedom.

The Art of War

Mandela did not choose violence at first. He began as a pacifist who preferred to use his wits and mind to win a battle. However, when it came to it, he knew he had to take up arms as others had before him. In the early 1960s, he made his decision by advocating a sabotage campaign. He founded the group "Spear of the Nation" in 1961. They were the militant wing of the African National Congress.

Once Nelson Mandela decided to take up arms and fight alongside his people, he quickly became a master in the arts of disguise and evasion. Mandela was given the nickname the Black Pimpernel for his ability to escape capture and arrest. His skill soon became legendary.

Mandela would frequently disguise himself in order to blend in or pass by others unnoticed. His most popular disguises were as a chef, fieldworker, and chauffeur. A little-known fact is that Mandela was disguised as a chauffeur when he was finally captured. In 1962, Mandela was driving with Cecil Williams, a fellow activist, when he was apprehended. He was wearing his chauffeur disguise at the time, but he mentioned that the moment he saw a Ford V-8 filled with white men shoot past them, he knew his life as a man on the run was over.

A Life in Prison

Upon his arrest, Nelson Mandela remained strong and determined. He stood in front of the court and proclaimed his love for his cause. He openly stated that he was not afraid to die for what he believed in. It was his willingness to die for his cause that saved his life. Instead of sentencing him to death, he was given life in prison.

While in prison, Mandela discovered a talent for passing around secret notes. He was incarcerated on the infamous Robben Island, and while there, he and the other prisoners used hidden and secret notes in order to communicate. They would leave the notes in matchboxes, taped in toilet tanks, and hidden under piles of dishes.

These messages weren't just a way to communicate while imprisoned. Mandela used them in order to continue his struggle. Through the notes, he managed to arrange a hunger strike with the other prisoners in an effort to improve all of their living conditions. Robben Island is known for its cruel conditions and harsh environment. Even while he was in prison, Nelson Mandela refused to stand idly by while his people suffered. The hunger strike was successful, and the prisoners earned themselves some better living conditions.

The armed struggle continued outside the prison. Nelson Mandela could not join his people in the struggle, but they would not rest just because he was imprisoned. Because of this, he was offered a deal.

In 1985, P.W. Botha, South African President at the time, offered Nelson Mandela his freedom if he agreed to renounce the armed struggle. Mandela did not even consider the deal, knowing that the freedom he was being offered was not freedom at all. In his reply he stated, "Only free men can negotiate. A prisoner cannot enter into contracts."

He remained in prison until his sentence came to an end 27 years later.

A Man of Peace

Nelson Mandela was ready for a war against the oppressors, but he fought just as hard for peace as he did for freedom. Prior to the ANC's eventual triumph, the people of South Africa feared that the country would fall into a civil war. It seemed inevitable due to the constant struggle between the different powers of the country.

Instead of the mass acts of retribution that everyone expected when Nelson Mandela and his party succeeded, Mandela instead established the Truth and Reconciliation Commission. This was done to peacefully investigate any human rights abuses that occurred under the Apartheid law and punish them accordingly. This succeeded in serving justice where it was due, pleasing the people while also avoiding any bloodshed.

After winning his struggle, he also worked to improve the lives of his people. According to his biography, at the end of Mandela's administration, he connected three million people to safe drinking water, brought education to 1.5 million children, upgraded or built 500 clinics, connected 2 million people to the electricity grid, and built 750,000 houses that provided shelter for around 3 million people.

Nelson Mandela cared for his people, and his struggle never ended. Even after ending Apartheid and winning the freedom of his people, he still struggled to improve their lives and help his country recover from the rift that tore it apart.

Lessons From a Man of Wisdom and Peace

"It always seems impossible until it's done."

- Nelson Mandela

Mandela is a man who spent his life struggling for the freedom of his people, going to prison for 27 years, and finally freeing an entire nation through his struggle. He is a man of peace and a man of wisdom. There is so much he taught the world, and there is still more that leaders can learn from him on their journey to greatness.

Passion Is Perseverance

Nelson Mandela had a cause that he knew was worth fighting for. He had a passion for it, and that passion fueled him. It fueled his perseverance. He opposed his country's government, and his passion led him along his path.

If he didn't have the passion he needed, he would have given up on his struggle. He wouldn't have fought as hard as he did. He would have taken that deal to be released from prison. He would have simply turned away from his people's suffering and continued with his own life as best he could.

Passion is perseverance, and without it, nothing that needs to be done can be done. All great leaders need a passion for their cause. You need to want to see your dream be realized no matter what. You need that passion to carry you through the struggle.

Passion is also contagious, as Nelson Mandela showed through his struggle. His followers saw his passion and knew he would fight no matter what. This inspired them to follow him and show the same amount of passion for the cause.

A great leader needs to have a burning passion to see his vision realized and to help him carry his followers along the path to that vision. No challenge is too much, and no struggle is too hard when you have the perseverance born from a pure passion for what you believe in.

Forgiveness

Nelson Mandela struggled for most of his life to win the freedom of his people from South Africa's oppressive government. They stole 27 years from him by throwing him in a cruel and harsh jail as punishment for wanting nothing more than the rights and freedom of his people. He had every right to feel hatred and anger towards the people who stole his life. Any other man would have sought revenge the moment he received his victory, but not a great man.

Bill Clinton, who was the American president at the time of Nelson Mandela's release from prison, once had a meeting with him. He stated that upon watching the news on the day of Mandela's release from prison, he noticed hatred and anger on Mandela's face. The moment he walked out of the prison gates and the cameras zoomed in on him, Clinton spotted his hatred towards the people who stole his years, but in an instant, that hatred was gone.

54

Nelson Mandela's emotions naturally gravitated towards resentment, hatred, and anger for the people who took those 27 years away from him, but he decided to make a different choice. He understood that pain and suffering were unavoidable. Things happen. Leadership changes, tsunamis wipe out entire cities, friends fall ill, employees fail, and people die. There is no way to avoid struggle in your life, one way or another.

Forgiveness is the only thing that can carry you through all of this. You cannot control everything, but you can choose to control your emotions. Forgive those that fail or betray you. Forgive the world, for it is not perfect. Understand that after forgiveness comes change, and change is something you can control.

Change Is Messy

Change is the driving force in this world. Everything is changing all of the time. Some things change for the better, some things change for the worse, and sometimes you can control the change you see in the world. The most important thing to remember is that change can be messy.

Change is often difficult and filled with misfortune, sacrifice, and pain. Change cannot come easily. There will be people who fight against change. There will be things standing in the way of change. Sometimes the things you want to change never can, while the things you want to stay the same are always changing.

Nelson Mandela knew that he could change the world if he fought hard enough, but he understood that the change he wanted would not come easy. He expected it to be hard. He knew it would be painful. He prepared himself and others for it.

If you wish to bring about change, you must be prepared for whatever mess that change will come with. Change is not impossible, but it is not easy.

Cooperation

Nelson Mandela knew above all else that he could not bring about change by himself. He could not force his enemy into defeat, and he could not hope to win his victory alone. The oppressive government that put his people through suffering and locked him away in a prison for 27 years was not only his enemy; they were also a means to an end.

Mandela focused on ending right and not being right. Being right is about a man's ego and pride. Being right is about humiliating your opponent and focusing on the past. However, ending right focuses on the future and what you wish to achieve from your struggle. Being right is nothing compared to ending right.

Nelson Mandela believed in being strong and fighting hard, but he also believed in being kind and humble. He once said, "No one is more dangerous than one who is humiliated." Through this, he understood that he could not make peace with his enemies if he wasn't willing to work with them.

Whether you're dealing with a partner, customer, or employee, you have to know what your motive is. Is your motive to become closer to them? To come to an agreement? To have both sides of the party emerge stronger? To have them understand your goals and you understand theirs? Or is your motive simply to win the argument?

Learning to compromise is the difference between a poor leader and a great man.

Self-Awareness

Nelson Mandela mentioned that his 27 years in prison were more than just a struggle for freedom and punishment for doing so. He found a silver lining to all of those wasted years. It gave him the time he needed to look inside himself and create in him what he wanted to see in the world. He wanted to build a South Africa that was filled with equality, peace, freedom, reconciliation, and harmony. He knew that he could not expect to see those qualities in the world he was trying to build unless he created those same qualities within himself.

How can he be a man who fights for peace when there is no peace within him? How can he search for harmony and freedom when he is imprisoned by his internal turmoil? Nelson Mandela took his 27 years of imprisonment and used them to look at himself in the mirror and change those qualities about himself. Change starts from within.

Self-awareness is a sign of any great leader. If you want to lead your followers into change, you have to be the change you wish to see. You cannot expect something from your followers if you do not expect the same thing from yourself. The person you choose to be and the person you show to your followers will affect the people they choose to become.

Great leadership is something that is passed down through generations. You have to ask yourself: What are you leaving behind? What stories will they tell of you? How will you be remembered? The legacy you leave is what will influence your followers. The person you choose to be will determine the change you will make.

5

Winston Churchill - The Man Who Led the World in Its Most Painful Time

"Success is not final, failure is not fatal: it is the courage to continue that counts."

- Winston Churchill

Winston Churchill is a long-remembered name throughout human history. He was charged with leading the Allied powers and Britain through one of the largest and most devastating battles in history: World War II. He used wisdom and persistence to lead his men from the brink of defeat all the way to their eventual victory. The Second World War was one of the most brutal battles of the 20th century, and it was Winston Churchill's great character that led the world through this traumatic time.

He is by far one of the world's greatest leaders and greatest men.

The World's Greatest Battle and the Man Who Led Us to Victory

Winston Churchill had many achievements in his life. He was a writer, statesman, orator, and leader. He was born in 1874 in Oxfordshire to rich, aristocratic ancestry. Churchill received a high education, although he never managed to achieve high grades while in school, but he had an early fascination with the military that led to him joining the Royal Cavalry in 1895.

Winston Churchill spent time as a soldier and a part-time journalist. He traveled the world. His trips took him to far corners of the world, including Egypt, Cuba, South Africa, and Afghanistan. He became a cultured man and a man who was used to a fight.

Before World War II, which started in 1939, Churchill had warned about Hitler and the rise of Nazi Germany. He saw the disaster coming before many others could. Before the war began, he saw himself in and out of office on a constant basis. In 1900, he was elected Conservative

MP for Oldham, but in 1904 he defected to the Liberal Party. He spent the next decade working his way up the ranks of the Liberal government. He was given the title of First Lord of the Admiralty and served as the civil/political head of the Royal Navy. He resigned from this position after the disaster of the Gallipoli campaign, which was of his creation. It was a great failure and resulted in the loss of millions of lives. He was heavily criticized for his error, so he chose to resign and traveled to the Western Front, where he fought back the Ottoman Empire.

Churchill crossed the floor once again from the Liberal Party to the Conservative Party. He made many controversial decisions during this time. He opted for Britain to rejoin the Gold Standard, and he had a firm opposition to Indian Independence. However, despite these controversial ideas, he was right in his warning against the appeasement of Nazi Germany when World War II eventually broke out in 1939.

In 1940, Neville Chamberlain resigned from his position as Prime Minister, and Winston Churchill was chosen to succeed him. He was Prime Minister of an all-party coalition government as the entire nation came together to fight the war.

During his time as Prime Minister, Churchill also created the position of Minister of Defense and appointed himself to that position. He became active in both diplomatic and administrative functions as he prosecuted the British war effort.

Churchill was most well known for his speeches, as he used them to build morale during the hardest times of the war. Some of the most memorable speeches that he ever gave were given during this time period.

It became clear how essential Winston Churchill's leadership was to winning the war when he lost the General Election in 1945. The Labour leader, Clement Attlee, won the election, and Churchill was out of office. However, he did not stop contributing to the war effort. He instead concentrated on public speaking in order to raise morale. During this period, he gave his most famous speech of all time in 1946. He declared that "an iron curtain has descended across the continent." This speech was meant to warn the people of the danger of Soviet Russia as it continued to rise in power.

In 1951, the re-election saw Winston Churchill back into office. He retook his position as Prime Minister, but in the words of Roy Jenkins, he was "gloriously unfit for office."

Winston Churchill was an aging man, and his health was increasingly worsening. He often conducted business from his bed because his health was too poor for him to leave it. Still, even in this state, Churchill prevailed and led the country through its most trying times. They won the war and pushed back the power of Nazi Germany. Churchill's powerful personality, oratory abilities, and wisdom of war endured despite his poor health.

With the war over he could rest, but the cold war that followed it would not allow this. Unfortunately, his leadership skills were a lot less decisive during this period. His second term in office saw the Consecutive Party's acceptance of Labour's Welfare State that they newly created. Due to this, Churchill had limited effect on domestic policy.

His attempts at stopping the Cold War from developing through his personal diplomacy failed him, and his poor health continued to hold him back. This saw the end of Winston Churchill's leadership. He resigned in 1955 and made way for Anthony Eden, his Foreign Secretary and Deputy Prime Minister, to succeed him.

Winston Churchill's poor health led to his death in 1965, and he was honored with a state funeral. He was a great leader; even towards the end of his life, he tried his best to help his country through its hardships.

Inspiring Times and Hardships

"Now this is not the end. It is not even the beginning of the end. But it is, perhaps, the end of the beginning."

\- Winston Churchill

A Lonely Child Becomes a Great Man

Winston Churchill was born to a rich family. His parents were Lord Randolph Churchill and Jennie Jerome. His mother was the daughter of an American millionaire, Leonard Jerome. As a child, he had access to all material comforts, and he never had to know a cold night or an empty stomach. However, throughout his childhood, he was deprived of one thing: parental affection.

With both of his parents being prestigious members of society, they were often swept up in worldly affairs. They never had time for their son, so they were rarely around him as he grew up. All Churchill had was his nanny, Mrs. Elizabeth Anne Everest, who also doubled as his confidant and his playmate. She was entrusted with supervising Winston Churchill as a child, but she also became his only friend.

At the age of 7, Churchill was sent off to boarding school, throwing him into an even deeper loneliness. He never performed well in his early years at school. He received poor grades and failed constantly. He received much wrath from his tutors and, most of all, from his parents.

His father repeatedly berated him. His father would constantly state that Churchill would grow up to be a failure, dampening his spirits and making it harder for him to better himself at school.

At a young age, Churchill became used to the fact that he would never have a genial relationship with his parents. He used to send letters to his mother often, begging her to visit him at school, but she never did. Neither of his parents ever visited him at school. He was a lonely child, and he had grown used to that fact early on.

Despite his poor grades and trouble in school, Churchill showed that he had a great memory early on. He once demonstrated his powerful memory when he won an award for reciting a poem that was 1,200 lines long.

His later years at school saw him shine and come into his own. He started excelling at his work, improving steadily, and earning better grades. He joined sports teams and even became his school's fencing champion. It was during this time that he began studying politics. At first, he studied it from a philosophical point of view as he tried to understand and define natural justice and natural rights. Later, he would study it from a contemporary point of view. He scrutinized the political conditions faced by many countries all around the world, and he saw an opportunity for change.

As a child, his father wanted Churchill to join the infantry, but when he left school, Churchill joined the cavalry. The grade requirements for joining were low enough that he could get accepted, even with his poor history in academics, and it didn't require him to learn math, which was a subject that Churchill hated with a passion. Therefore, Churchill left his lonely childhood behind and began his climb to become one of the greatest men in history.

A Teller of Stories

Winston Churchill was a multi-talented man. He kept himself busy with multiple interests, and he made a point at excelling in all of them. He was a painter, a writer, a poet, a war correspondent, a politician, and a war leader.

His fling with literature is what he is most well-known for, as it sparked his ability to deliver powerful and inspiring speeches. He began by signing up as a war correspondent. He did this mainly to add extra income to the small amount he made as a soldier early on in his war career. He has his name on many different works: *The River War*, *The Story of Malakand Field Force*, six volumes of World War II, and four volumes of accounts of World War I are all established works of Churchill's as a war correspondent.

He wrote *Savrola*, his only work of fiction, but he is known better for his war correspondence and for the biography he wrote on his father, Lord Randolph Churchill. Other works he is known for are *The Unrelenting Struggle*, *History of English Speaking Peoples*, and *The Dawn of*

Liberation and Victory. In 1953, he was awarded the Nobel Prize for Literature.

Aside from his talented writing, he was also an avid painter, painting over 500 canvases in his lifetime. His multiple talents and genius as a politician all worked together to make him the great leader that he was. He had passion for all of his interests, and that passion made his character one that others wanted to follow.

Lessons for Life and Greatness From a War Leader

"You have enemies? Good. That means you've stood up for something, sometime in your life."

- Winston Churchill

During his lifetime, Winston Churchill never backed down from a challenge, he never let anyone or anything discourage him, and he was always eager to teach those who wanted to learn a lesson. He was the commander of words and the genius of war. He had wisdom, knowledge, and a powerful character. The lessons he taught during his life can still be learned today by those seeking the same greatness that he found.

Words Are Powerful

Winston Churchill was an artist not only with paint and vision but also with his words. He understood the power that words had, and he knew how to use that power. Words, when used correctly, can have an emotional impact that actions could never achieve. For this reason, word choice mattered to Churchill.

On one occasion, during World War II, he was discussing strategy with the British General Harold Alexander where the general referred to Germany as "Hitler's European Fortress." Upon hearing this, Churchill grew angry at the general and yelled out, "Never use that term again. Never use that term again!"

Because Churchill knew how powerful words could be, he knew that if the term "Hitler's European Fortress" was ever heard by the public, it would strike fear into their hearts. The very image it would create in their minds would put a stop to their will to fight. A term such as that could only work to Hitler's advantage.

In 1940, when Churchill was worried that the German army would attempt to invade England, the Ministry of Information wanted to send a message to the people that simply stated, "stay put." Churchill was unhappy with this choice of words and instead told him to say, "Stand Firm." A simple change like this can empower the people and give them a sense of strength.

Churchill preferred old words to new ones, believing they carried more strength. One example is how he never referred to Germany as their enemy. He only ever used the word "foe." Words are strong, and the way you use them can either mean victory or defeat.

A Leader Is Self-Made

One of the things we can learn from Winston Churchill is that the greatest of leaders often make themselves. His leadership skills were not given to him by someone else. It was not part of the wisdom given to him by a teacher who believed in him or a parent who wanted to see him succeed. Leadership was something he sought out and found himself.

Leaders can be taught, but it takes someone who actually wants to learn. As the quote goes, "You can take a horse to water, but you can not make it drink." Churchill saw success in himself and worked towards that. He didn't know what he had to do; all he knew was what he needed to do, and he did it. The sign of a true leader is someone who sees what needs to be done and doesn't hesitate to do it.

Follow Your Moral Compass

Winston Churchill had a moral compass that was sharper than anyone else's, and he followed it no matter what. Even when the divide between the north and the south in the United States happened, he made a moral case for defending Western values. His actions and thoughts were often the subject of controversy and scrutiny, but that didn't stop him from doing and thinking what he thought was right.

Following his moral compass led him down many paths. He knew that the Allies would win the war, but he still reflected on how perilous the whole situation was. He knew how high the stakes were for both his generation and all the future generations to come, but still, his moral compass told him that the Allies would win.

Winston Churchill understood morals far more than anyone else did. He understood that everyone else is in the middle of a moral struggle that will eventually define their life and who they are. He cautioned most against denying their moral compass.

He once said, "The only guide to a man is his conscience." Our conscience tells us what is right and what is wrong. It guides us through the difficult trials of life and helps us through our journey. Follow your moral compass. Let it point the way. You may be wrong more often than you are right, but you will always be certain about the way you need to go.

Think for Yourself

Winston Churchill was always an independent thinker. He didn't rely on others to tell him what he needed to do. He took initiative and thought on his feet. When he was out of power in the 1930s, he still recognized the threat that Nazi Germany posed to Britain, but he was unable to do anything about it since he was not in the government anymore. However, he still called for British rearmament, knowing that someone needed to say something if those in power weren't going to do anything.

The reason for this kind of thinking was that World War I was thought of as "the war to end all wars," and so many thought that Europe had entered into a long period of peace. Even as the Nazi Powers rose in Germany, the British government didn't want to believe that another war was on the way.

Winston Churchill didn't follow this thinking and instead, he thought for himself. He watched Germany invest heavily in the military, and he called for Britain to do the same.

His lesson to other leaders is to think for yourself and don't wait for others to think for you. Don't follow the masses and what they think might happen. Followers listen to the thoughts of others, while leaders will trust and follow their own thoughts.

6

Albert Einstein - The Man Who Rewrote the Laws of Nature

"If you can't explain it to a six-year-old, you don't understand it yourself."

- Albert Einstein

Albert Einstein is one of the most famous scientists of the 20th century. He had a profound impact on how we understand the universe, light, time, and gravity. He changed the course of human history and rewrote the laws of nature. To this day, his work has guided us along the path to new frontiers and helped us understand our standing and significance in the universe.

The Man Who Understood the Universe

Albert Einstein is known as the genius of the 20th century and the man who rewrote the laws of nature. He is also called the father of the atomic bomb and blamed for its creation. This is, however, a false fact about the genius that shaped our modern world. Albert Einstein's only hand in the creation of the atomic bomb was a letter he sent to President Franklin D. Roosevelt that encouraged the U.S. to build the atomic bomb before the Germans could succeed in doing so. He later stated that he only did so because he thought the Germans were close to creating one. He also said that if he knew they weren't close to the creation of an atomic bomb, he would have said nothing about it.

Albert Einstein's more notable accomplishments have given scientists information about our universe that helped mankind go into space. Thanks to him, we know more about the stars that shine millions of miles away as well as our Sun and Earth.

Among his greatest achievements are his contributions to four major areas of science: time, light, energy, and gravity. He published four scientific papers in 1905, one in each of these areas of science. This was the year that is referred to by today's scientists as Einstein's miracle year.

These four major areas of science were significantly advanced when Albert Einstein published these papers. The advances he made helped scientists after him make even more advances and understand our universe better.

He gave an explanation regarding the dynamics of individual moving bodies. He explained the nature of time and space. He explained that light energy came in quanta or chunks that are now referred to as photons. Without this explanation, researchers would never have thought about the nature of light the way they do now. Finally, he explained Brownian motion, which helped prove that molecules exist.

His many accomplishments also include finally explaining why the sky was blue. In 1910, he finally managed to answer the question that many asked about the sky by explaining the critical opalescence phenomenon and the effect of the scattering of light by the molecules in the atmosphere.

In 1921, the Nobel Prize in Physics was awarded to Albert Einstein "for his services to theoretical physics and especially for his discovery of the law of the photoelectric effect." The Royal Society awarded him the Copley Medal in 1925, which is the oldest scientific award still surviving in the world. He received many other awards, including the Matteucci Medal in 1921, the Gold Medal of the Royal Astronomical Society in 1926, the Max Planck Medal in 1929, and the Franklin Medal in 1935. This makes him one of the most awarded scientists in history, and in 1999, he was named the Person of the Century by Time Magazine.

Albert Einstein was also very influential in promoting the Israeli state. He openly promoted liberty and freedom of thought in a time that was filled with hatred and racism. He dared to stand against the thoughts and ideals of others. He truly did change the shape of the world and how we see it.

Logic and Imagination

"Logic will get you from A to Z; imagination will get you everywhere."

\- Albert Einstein

Albert Einstein's childhood was filled with imagination, and he grew up into a man of knowledge and logic. His amazing stories of discovery and learning are a source of inspiration for everyone. His ability to see what others could not see put him in a position to change the world and change the world he did.

Discovering Light

Albert Einstein's fascination with logic mixed with his imagination at an early age. It started with his fascination with light. At the age of 16, he often wondered what it would be like if he could ride his bike on a beam of light. He wondered about this, but that was all he could do until only ten years later.

In 1905, he had something that he referred to as a "Thought Experiment," and he came up with a theory of relativity. In this theory, he stated that light is constant. Until this point, scientists believed light to be a wavelike picture like time, but his theory would prove them all wrong.

Along with this theory, he also came up with the thought that nothing can travel faster than the speed of light, which he theorized was 186,000 miles/second. He also stated that light travels at the same speed all the time. It doesn't matter if the light is coming from the headlight of a train that is speeding down the train tracks or if the light is coming from a lantern shining down the tracks. The light itself will always travel at the same speed no matter what.

His theory of nothing being able to travel faster than the speed of light was proven right with lightning. The crack of lightning is visible before the sound of thunder because light travels faster than even sound.

In the same year, Einstein stated in a theory that light's speed is constant, but that time is not constant. He stated that the faster someone goes the slower time moves for them, even though it does not feel as though time is moving slower for that person.

A Man of Math

It's a well-known fact that Albert Einstein failed at math, and many children have used this fact to find solace in their hatred for the subject. However, this could not be further from the truth. Albert did not fail at math, nor did he hate the subject. The records show that he was an exceptional student in all of his subjects, even if he was a little reluctant when it came to math.

Einstein scored highly in all of his subjects during his school days, and the only thing that truly frustrated him was the "mechanical discipline" that he described the teachers demanded. He did eventually drop out of school at the age of 15, but it had nothing to do with his inability to achieve acceptable grades.

He lived in Germany as a child, where it was a state mandate that children of a certain age sign up for military service. At the age of 15, Einstein dropped out of school and left Germany in order to avoid this, but before that, he was always at the top of his class. His teachers even considered him to be a prodigy since he was able to grasp complex scientific and mechanical concepts.

For years, underachieving children have used the false fact that a genius such as Albert Einstein dropped out of school and did poorly in math to make their poor grades look better, but it simply isn't true.

A Subject of the FBI's Fascination

Albert Einstein was spied on by the FBI for over two decades. In 1933, shortly after Hitler rose to power, Einstein had left Berlin for New Jersey in the United States and took up a position at the Institute for Advanced Study in Princeton. Before this, Einstein openly supported civil rights, pacifist actions, and left-wing causes. This drew the suspicion of J. Edgar Hoover, an FBI agent. When Einstein arrived on American shores, appearing to be escaping Hitler's rise to power, he became the center of a 22-year-long surveillance campaign.

For years, FBI agents listened to his phone calls, rooted through his trash, opened up his mail, and watched him on a constant basis, all in an attempt to unmask him as a Soviet spy. They even followed up on tips that he was building a death ray.

The surveillance project did not reveal anything, but by the time of Albert Einstein's death, his FBI file was at least 1,800 pages long.

The Story of Regret

Towards the end of the 1930s, Albert Einstein made a decision that he would regret for the rest of his life. He learned of new research that had put the German scientists working for Hitler on a path that would lead them to the creation of the atom bomb. Einstein knew of the power of the bomb. He knew that it could bring about a doomsday, and the thought of it being in the hands of the Nazis scared him. He became convinced that it was time to set aside his pacifist principles, and he created a team with Leo Szilard, a Hungarian physicist.

Together they wrote a letter to Franklin D. Roosevelt, President of the United States at the time, expressing their concerns about Germany creating an atomic bomb. They urged the president to conduct his own research and create one first. The president heeded their warning and started the Manhattan Project which would eventually lead to the creation of the first atomic bomb.

Einstein never participated in the Manhattan Project, nor did he assist in creating the bomb himself. However, after its creation and the destruction it caused during the war, he expressed deep regrets about the minor role he played in its creation.

He stated that had he known the Germans would not have succeeded in creating an atomic bomb themselves, he would never have lifted a finger. His regret for playing a role in the bomb's creation fueled his passion for advocating for nuclear disarmament. He also advocated for a unified world government and controls on weapons testing.

Einstein and Bertrand Russell signed the "Russell-Einstein Manifesto," which was a public letter that brought to light and stressed the risks of nuclear war and implored the world's governments to instead find peaceful means for the settlement of all their disputes rather than start a war that could end the world.

A Presidential Request

Although Einstein was never a traditionally religious man, he always felt a deep connection to his Jewish heritage. He often spoke against anti-Semitism. Einstein was never a staunch Zionist, but he never denounced religion altogether. When Chaim Weizmann, the head of state of Israel, died in 1952, the Israeli government was quick to offer Albert Einstein a position as the second president of the nation.

At the time, he was already 73 years old, and he was quick to decline the offer. Although it was an honor, he had no interest in becoming a president. He wrote them a letter in response saying, "All my life I have dealt with objective matters, hence I lack both the natural aptitude and the experience to deal properly with people and to exercise official function." With this letter that he wrote to the Israeli ambassador, he turned down their offer to be the country's second president, showing his humbleness and his ability to witness his own strengths and weaknesses.

A Fun Guy

Probably the most famous image of Albert Einstein is the one where he is sticking his tongue out at the camera, and no one can forget his iconic wild hair. Albert Einstein was a man who enjoyed the little things in life, like being silly. He was a fun person to have around, and he was never too serious.

Albert Einstein's desire to be silly and act childish can teach us all a lesson. He was always in touch with his inner child, and he said that made him better. Children have an abundance of curiosity and aren't afraid to be proven wrong, so they don't mind chasing down theories or asking questions. Einstein credited his ability to ask questions, seek answers, and see patterns where no one else could to his inner child that he was so in touch with.

Being silly, having a fun time, and acting childish every now and again does not mean you're unfit for leadership. Albert Einstein proved that a child's mind can show an interesting viewpoint on any subject.

An Unusual Brain

Albert Einstein's death in 1955 came at a ripe old age. He had requested cremation for his body after his death, but Thomas Harvey, a Princeton pathologist, removed Einstein's brain during his autopsy and kept it. He hoped that through research on the brain, they could unlock the secrets of his genius.

Thomas Harvey sought approval from Einstein's son, and he reluctantly gave Harvey his approval. Harvey was quick to have Einstein's brain cut up into pieces and then had those pieces sent off to various scientists to conduct their research.

Since the 1980s, a handful of studies have been conducted on the brain, but all of them have been discredited or dismissed one way or another. The most famous of these studies came in 1999 when a team of scientists from a Canadian university published a paper claiming that Albert Einstein's brain had unusual folds on his parietal lobe. This part of the brain is mostly associated with spatial and mathematical ability, but this study has yet to be proven or discredited.

The secrets of Einstein's genius have yet to be unlocked, and to this day his brain remains a mystery to all.

Lessons From a Genius

"Strive to not be a success, but rather to be of value."

- Albert Einstein

Albert Einstein was a leading scientist and one of the greatest men of the 20th century. He followed his curiosity and let his imagination drive him. He was not only a man of wisdom and logic but a man of invention and wittiness. He led the world into a new era of science and understanding. He was a leader unlike any other and a great man with a great legacy.

The Present Is Important, so Focus On It

Albert Einstein was misunderstood as focusing on the future when he was really focusing on the present. He once said that if a man is able to drive a car at the same time as kissing a woman, then he is not giving the kiss the attention it deserves.

He believed that people could build a bright future for the generations to come, but he also believed that focusing on the present was the way to build that bright future. In other words, if your focus is on the future, then you cannot truly focus on the present. Splitting your focus between the two of them will result in harming one of the other.

Living strongly and fully in the present is the best and only way to build a bright future.

Imagination Is a Powerful Thing

We all know that Einstein's imagination, coupled with his intelligence, was his most powerful tool. If it weren't for his imagination, he wouldn't have come up with any of his theories. He needed to imagine the scenarios before he could put any logic to them.

You need imagination in order to reach your goals. You need to build the world you want with your imagination in order to see it built in front of you.

Mistakes Are Gifts

Einstein always thought of mistakes as gifts that can better you. He never believed in a perfect plan or a perfect theory. Mistakes are inevitable. Instead of trying to avoid mistakes and regretting ever making one, Einstein saw mistakes as an opportunity to learn.

"Mistakes become the essence of their genius," Einstein said about successful people. So take pride in your mistakes and focus heavily on them. If you can learn from your mistakes and better yourself, it makes it worth having them.

Live in the Moment

Albert Einstein taught us to live in the moment. Time flies by, and you can miss any moment that flies by with it. Each moment of your life brings life lessons or valuable pieces of experience that will change the way you see and interact with the world.

Live in the moment. Don't focus on what you need to do tomorrow and end up missing what you did today. Focus on what's happening around you right now.

7

Stephen Hawking - The Man Who Triumphed Over All Limitations

"Intelligence is the ability to adapt to change."

\- Stephen Hawking

Stephen Hawking was a huge inspiration for everyone, including those with disabilities. Before Stephen Hawking, disabilities were seen as a hurdle in someone's life. People with disabilities were held back and couldn't compete with others, but Stephen Hawking put a stop to that kind of thinking.

He was a renowned cosmologist, physicist, and author. He was the first scientist to explain the theory of cosmology and is best known for his unique origins of the universe.

The Theory of Everything

"Quiet people have the loudest minds."
- Stephen Hawking

In 2018, Stephen Hawking died at the age of 76 after living a long life that many told him he would not be able to have. To this day, Stephen Hawking is one of the world's most recognizable scientists. He holds an iconic status that he can never lose.

He was a multi-talented genius. He has many books published, has appeared on different television shows, has changed the way we see the universe in more ways than any scientist since Albert Einstein, and has routinely stunned everyone with his incredible personality and sense of humor.

He left behind two legacies: his scientific legacy and the legacy of his life. His disability and his cultural status often overshadowed his scientific breakthroughs. It was a shame that the genius of the man who developed the theory of everything had his brilliant mind lost in the mess of his unique and difficult life.

Hawking's scientific career began in 1962 at the University of Cambridge, where he began his PhD. Hawking's career began in disappointment. Hawking would have a supervisor while at the university, but his chosen supervisor, Fred Hoyle, already had a full complement of students and could not take another one. At the time, Fred Hoyle was one of the most famous British astrophysicists, and this meant that he was a magnet for some of the most ambitious students. Hawking was disappointed by this, but it was by far the least of his troubles.

In the same year, Hawking received a diagnosis of amyotrophic lateral sclerosis. The degenerative motor neurone disease quickly works through the victim's body and robs them of their ability to voluntarily move any of their muscles. At that point, Stephen Hawking was told that he only had two years to live.

Hawking's body was weakening on a daily basis, but his mind and intellect continued to grow and stay sharp. He continued to feed his intellect and work towards his PhD. Two years later, his body was weak. He found difficulty in talking and walking, but at this point, it became clear to him and others that the disease was progressing much slower than they had originally feared.

The news of his disease's slow progression, along with his engagement to Jane Wilde, renewed his desire and passion to progress in physics. Hawking began his PhD working under Dennis Sciama, a physicist that Hawking did not know before they began working together. Working with her had its advantages. Hoyle's fame meant that he was always busy and seldom able to discuss anything with his students, but Hawking did not run into this problem with Sciama. She was always around, and she was eager to talk. This helped to stimulate Hawking's mind and helped him pursue his scientific vision.

Hawking's fascination surrounded the big bang theory and the beginning of time. The fact that he was put with Sciama instead of Hoyle worked more in his favor. Hoyle did not believe in the theory of the big bang; in fact, he actually coined the term "big bang" as a mockery of the theory. However, Sciama was happy to allow Hawking to investigate the beginning of time.

Stephen Hawking was interested in many of the theories that Albert Einstein was famous for. The main theory he investigated was the general theory of everything. Hawking spent his time studying Roger Penrose's work. His work proved that if the theory of everything was correct, then at the heart of every black hole, there must be a singularity; a space where time and space themselves break down. Hawking realized that the same reasoning could be used for the whole universe, and under Sciama's encouragement, he was able to work out the math and prove it. This was his first great achievement: proving that the universe, according to general relativity, also began as a singularity.

Hawking did not believe that Einstein had the last word. He believed that general relativity, Einstein's theory, did not take quantum mechanics into account. Hawking took the link he found between Penrose's singularity and the singularity at the center of the big bang and used it to find what everyone was searching for: the origin of the universe.

This was only the start of Hawking's journey as he went about changing the way we see the universe. He was the first scientist to even attempt to do so since Albert Einstein first introduced his theories.

Stephen Hawking's contributions to the world of physics earned him several honors. The Royal Society elected him one of its youngest fellows in 1974. In 1977, he became the professor of gravitational physics at Cambridge, and then in 1979, he was appointed to the Lucasian professorship of mathematics at Cambridge. This was a post previously held by Isaac Newton.

In 1982, he was made a Commander of the Order of the British Empire, and in 1989, he was also made a Companion of Honor. The Royal Society gave him the Copley Medal in 2006, and in 2009, he received the U.S. Presidential Medal of Freedom. Among these many honors, he also accepted a visiting research chair at the Perimeter Institute for Theoretical Physics in 2008.

Stephen Hawking left this world a man of many accomplishments. He changed so much about our universe, and to this day, physicists are still using his genius to guide their own theories. He beat all odds and worked against all limitations. His body gave out on him, but his mind continued to grow and nourish his thoughts. He was the leading scientist for many decades, and even in his death, he is still a leader in his field. He was a great man who let nothing and no one stand in his way.

A Brilliant Mind Trapped in a Prison

"Although I cannot move and I have to speak through a computer, in my mind I am free."

- Stephen Hawking

Stephen Hawking was a man who beat the odds. He lived longer than anyone else ever thought that he could have and did more than anyone else thought he could have. His life was filled with accomplishments. He was a great man who let nothing stop him and proved to everyone that nothing can hold you back as long as you have the will.

Beating the Odds

At the age of 21, he was diagnosed with a horrible disease that would have his body slowly break down and bring his life expectancy down to almost nothing. The symptoms of such a disease would usually only develop in people aged 50 or older, and the disease would usually lead to death within only a few months or sometimes years.

When the doctors diagnosed Stephen Hawking with this disease at the age of 21, an extremely young age to get this disease, they predicted that he would only live for a couple of years. Hawking went on to marry his wife at the age of 26 and live to the ripe old age of 76.

His body gave out on him, but his will and mind never did. He said, "The human race is so puny compared to the universe that being disabled is not of much cosmic significance."

He saw the universe, and he knew it was larger than him or any issues he was dealing with. He knew there were mysteries out there that needed to be solved, and he could let nothing get in his way.

A Bad Driver

After his diagnosis in the 60s, he began using crutches. At first, he resisted transitioning to the use of a wheelchair for as long as possible, but when it came to it, and he had no choice, he was reportedly a pretty wild man behind the wheel.

There was a story circulating that he once ran over Prince Charles' toes when he got the chance to meet the Royal Family. Kristin M. Larsen, a professor in astronomy, said, "I don't know if it's true that he actually ran over Prince Charles' toes."

Kristin M. Larsen was also the author of *Stephen Hawking: A Biography*. In that book, she talks about the fun he would have on the dance floor. "He definitely liked to dance in his wheelchair on the dance floor," she said. She spoke about how he would whiz through a conference in his wheelchair, speeding around and having the time of his life. There was one incident where he went too fast and crashed his wheelchair, leading to a broken hip. Stephen Hawking was famous for being a jokester. Even after breaking his hip, he instantly joked about it, saying something along the lines of "being a bad driver."

A Controversial Thinker

When Hawking first presented his theories to his colleagues, they didn't think the same way he did. His scientific theories and understanding of the universe were controversial. He didn't let this stop him. He placed his bet on science, and he stuck to it as any betting man would have.

When he first presented his theory that black holes should radiate, his colleagues thought it was rubbish. They didn't believe it was possible, and they thought no rational thinking man would come up with such a theory. Stephen Hawking didn't let it end at that. He doubled down and presented them with his calculations for his theory. They found that it was indeed true. Under the right circumstances, according to physics as they understood it, black holes should evaporate, and they should radiate.

Hawking believed in his theories to a point where he simply couldn't back down, even if he was proven wrong in the end. Stephen Hawking is known for his theoretical contributions, but he was known for not always getting everything right the first time. He had a big reputation for placing bets and losing them on scientific concepts.

In 1975, he had a bet going with Kip Thorne that an astronomical object known as Cygnus X-1 was not a black hole. He also bet that information can and does get lost in a black hole, and he also bet $100 to someone that the Higgs boson particle would never be discovered. He eventually lost all three of these bets, but that didn't stop him from making more bets in the future.

Artificial Intelligence Was the Stuff of Nightmares

One of Stephen Hawking's beliefs was that developing better technology was the only way humans could continue to not only survive but also thrive. However, he was concerned about the pursuit of better technology and that it would eventually lead to artificial intelligence (A.I.). He perceived many dangers and problems that would come with the development of A.I. He predicted that A.I. would bring new ways for the few to be able to easily oppress the many and more powerful autonomous weapons. He also believed that A.I. would eventually develop a will of its own, and that will would conflict with our own. Hawking said on the subject, "The rise of powerful A.I. will be either the best, or the worst thing, ever to happen to humanity." It was a personal subject for him, as he benefited greatly from the advances that scientists made in the field, but he still feared any great advances that could eventually lead to artificial intelligence.

Hawking benefited from advances in this field to help him with his speech. His disability took his speech from him, and he used a device that could detect the movement in his cheek and translate it into sound. It was a machine with a learning algorithm that was able to detect his cheek movements and turn it into words. It gradually got quicker and better at translating what he was trying to say, learning his speech patterns. This is the very essence of artificial intelligence, and he benefited greatly from it.

Children and Books

Stephen Hawking is well known for the many books he wrote, most of them centering around his theories and scientific discoveries, but not many know of the children's books he wrote with his daughter.

Hawking was a family man, and he had several children to show for it. He loved his children as much as he loved science. He wrote five children's books with his daughter's help. The children's books combined both adventure and science in a way to get children engaged in the world of science. He knew that if his daughter loved it and learned something from it then other children would love it as well.

These books focused on George, a young boy who learns all about the universe by traveling around in it.

Lessons From the Man of the Universe

"Intelligence is the ability to adapt to change."

- Stephen Hawking

Stephen Hawking is known to the public for his many books and his theories about black holes, but he is known to other scientists in his field as a genius and a leader in physics. His qualities in his work as a physicist were what made him the man he is to the world, but his qualities as a leader were far more important.

He had many qualities that made him a great leader. These qualities would have seemed like poor personality traits, but he managed to turn them into leadership skills.

Stubbornness

Stubbornness is one of those qualities that can either be good or bad, depending on how it's used. Stephen Hawking was an extremely stubborn man, but it ended up being one of his best qualities.

He would be very stuck in his ways. He'd come up with a theory and stick to it, no matter how many people disagreed with him or denied his theories. His stubbornness didn't allow him to give up simply because others found it easy to do so. He would eventually prove all of them wrong and himself right.

Being stubborn when it's unreasonable can lead to poor leadership, but stubbornness, when used correctly, can help you on your way to greatness.

Curiosity Is Key

Stephen Hawking once said, "I'm just a child who has never grown up." He said his child-like curiosity helped him discover his theories. Children are always eager to learn in one way or another. They're always asking questions and pushing for answers.

A child's most used words are 'why' and 'how.' Stephen Hawking said that he would always be obsessed with asking why and how questions whenever possible, and he would eventually find the answers.

Curiosity is the key to greatness. Without it, you'll never have the courage to seek out new knowledge and push past the world you currently know into a new and better one.

Communication Is Your Most Powerful Tool

Stephen Hawking once explained how communication is what sets man apart from the beast, aside from imagination. For millions of years, man lived just like the animals did. With the power of imagination, mankind learned to talk and listen. With speech, the communication of ideas, logic, and wisdom were allowed to flourish. This enabled mankind to build impossible things by working together. Hawking believed that the world we have today would not exist if it weren't for mankind's ability to communicate. This makes communication one of the greatest abilities that mankind possesses.

Stephen Hawking lost his ability to communicate. His disease took away his words and his speeches. Even with his hatred and fear of A.I., he still opted to use a learning machine in order to help him communicate better.

Communication is what brings ideas to life and allows civilizations to build. Communication is not just about speaking but also about listening. Listening to other people's ideas is just as important as sharing your own. To be a great leader, you must be able to communicate properly with your followers by listening and speaking with them as your equals.

Uncertainty Is Unavoidable

The future only exists in our minds and as part of a spectrum of possibilities. We may know our past, and we may try to control our present, but the future is uncertain, and we can't be afraid of that.

You cannot avoid uncertainty. Stephen Hawking lived in uncertainty all of his life, ever since he was diagnosed with his horrible disease. He was given only two years to live, but as those two years came and went, everything became very uncertain for him. Instead of allowing that uncertainty to scare him, Hawking allowed it to fuel his passion.

He didn't know when his disease would finally kill him, and that uncertainty pushed him harder than ever. He worked like he would never work again. He laughed like he would never laugh again. He enjoyed every second of his life and lived it to its fullest.

So while uncertainty is unavoidable, it can also be your most powerful ally.

Don't Let Anyone Get You Down

Stephen Hawking had to deal with a lot of negativity and naysayers in his lifetime. It seemed every second person wanted to tell him that he couldn't do something or that he was wrong. He didn't listen to any of them.

If someone tries to tell you that you can't do what you need to do, ignore them. Go with your gut. Do what you think you need to do or what you want to do. You may end up being wrong, as Stephen Hawking was wrong a lot of the times he tried something new, but he didn't let that stop him, and neither should you.

Even if you're wrong, and even if multiple people tell you not to do it, do it anyway. You might end up being right. It might end up being the best decision you ever made. Do it or you'll regret it because even if you end up failing, you'll be wiser and stronger for doing it.

8

Mother Teresa - A Woman Determined to Ease the World's Suffering

"What you spend years building may be destroyed over-night; build it anyway."

- Mother Teresa

Mother Teresa left a large dent in the world with her devotion to helping the world's poorest and most vulnerable people. Her devotion was unforgettable and unwavering. She did what she could and never let anything stand in her way. She was a truly selfless woman. Her greatest achievements and stories of her life are lessons for all who wish to be great and the next world leader.

The Missionaries of Charity

"Do not wait for leaders; do it alone, person to person."

- Mother Teresa

Clad in white with a blue-bordered sari, Mother Teresa and her sisters of the Missionaries of Charity quickly became a symbol of compassion, love, and care for the whole world. They were selfless women who wanted not and needed not. Instead, they gave their skills and their time to those who needed it more.

Mother Teresa, born Agnes Gonxha Bojaxhiu in 1910, was raised in a family of devoted Catholics. They would pray every evening, and they went to church almost every single day. Her family was generous; they cared for the poor, and they helped the less fortunate as much as they could. These actions impacted Mother Teresa greatly in her young life.

Her mother was a housewife, and her father was a simple but successful and well-known contractor. They had three children, of which she was the youngest. She had a simple childhood that helped carve her into the woman she later became.

Mother Teresa found most of her teachings and inspiration in her mother Drana. Drana was a selfless woman that cared for her community and her neighbors. She took care of a widowed woman with six children and an alcoholic woman from the neighborhood. When Drana could not go to do so, Mother Teresa would go in her place. She would bathe the alcoholic women twice a day and help care for the six children because the grieving widow could not do it all herself. One day, when the widow died, they took the six children in and raised them as part of the family.

Mother Teresa needed to learn all she could from her mother because she lost her father at the age of nine. Drana was left to raise their three children and the six that she had taken in. Drana had to work hard, sewing wedding dresses and making embroidery in order to pay for her children's needs. At the same time, she managed to focus on their education and be there for them. Mother Teresa credited growing up in this kind of environment as the reason she became so selfless and caring.

At the age of 18, Mother Teresa made the decision to become a nun. She did so because she wanted nothing more than to serve the poorest of the poor and do so on behalf of God.

For two years, she lent her assistance to several religious retreats in Letnice, and this made it clear to her that she would be a missionary for India. In 1928, she left her home in Albania and was accompanied to the station by her friends, neighbors, schoolmates, and family. Everybody wept for her as she left them. She traveled to Ireland, where she would eventually join the Sisters of Loretto in Dublin. She spent only a year in Ireland before leaving once again to join the Loretto convent in the Indian city of Darjeeling.

Mother Teresa was also known as a teacher. From 1929 to 1948, she taught at St. Mary's High School in Calcutta. She witnessed poverty and suffering on the outside of the convent walls, and it made such a deep impression on her that she needed to do something. She would eventually seek permission to leave the convent walls and work among the poor people in the slums of Calcutta. In 1949 she finally received that permission from her superiors.

She had no funds and almost nothing to work with, but she began by starting an open-air school for the homeless children. Soon she had voluntary helpers, and she received the financial support she needed from several churches and authorities. With this help, it was possible for her to extend her work, and in 1950, she received approval to start her own order, which would become known around the world as the Missionaries of Charity. Their primary task was to care for and love those that nobody else was prepared to look after. In the same year, she also took up her Indian citizenship.

Once the sisterhood was established, they extended their work by opening up centers and clinics and cared for lepers by providing them with homes and care. Those that they cared for were destitute and dying, but that didn't stop Mother Teresa from caring for them. She said, "These people have lived like animals. At least they can die like human beings."

In 1963, the Missionaries of Charity formed a male branch of the society known as the Brothers of Charity.

Young women rushed to join her sisterhood, and by 1965, they were recognized by the Vatican as a Pontifical Congregation. Their work had quickly spread to over 50 centers scattered throughout India, and invitations to do the same soon came to them from countries all over the world. By 1998, the Missionaries of Charity had 615 Houses in 124 countries, with 4,400 professed sisters and 350 professed brothers.

They operated homes for those suffering from leprosy, AIDS, and tuberculosis. They ran soup kitchens, family counseling programs, schools, and orphanages. However, in 1990, Mother Teresa was forced to scale back her efforts. Her health was quickly declining, and she was unable to help the world as much as she could before. Her sisters and brothers continued her work in her absence.

Her health was declining due to a combination of her old age, the conditions she lived in, and how hard she worked herself traveling across the world and helping others. In 1989, she suffered a nearly fatal heart attack and needed to have a pacemaker implanted in her heart. With her health condition in mind, she asked that her sisters choose a successor for her. Sister Nirmala was selected as her successor in 1997, and in the same year, the "Angel of Mercy" died at 87 years old.

Even though Mother Teresa's physical body departed from this world, many of her followers and the people whose lives she touched know that her soul still lives on in her work and the legacy that she left behind. She was a great woman and a great leader. She continues to live in the hearts of those poor souls whose lives she made better with her selfless acts.

Angel of Mercy

"Discipline is the bridge between goals and accomplishment."

- Mother Teresa

Mother Teresa did so many great and selfless deeds in her lifetime that it is hard to choose which of her stories are more inspiring. She urged for the good of humanity in everyone to come out and for people to do their best to help others. She did not think of herself. She did not think of what she wanted, what she needed, or her safety or health. She knew that others needed her, and the amazing stories of her accomplishments are the reason she is known as the Angel of Mercy.

Savior of Children and Broker of Peace

In 1982, Israel's siege on Beirut began. The Israeli army was under the command of Ariel Sharon at the time as they circled West Beirut. The area was struck with ground and aerial bombardments, and the death toll totaled around 500, according to some reports. The deaths were mostly among civilians, and there were just as many wounded. In the middle of the besieged capital, there was no water or food, and many people in the area were without power.

Mother Teresa arrived quickly in Lebanon in a small Christian part of the country that had been spared by the war. She made her way there because of a call she received from Amal Makarem, who was horrified by the scene he witnessed that he described as being worthy of Dante's inferno. The sight was that of mentally and physically disabled children abandoned and trapped in an orphanage in the western part of Beirut. They were without food, hygiene, or care. Some of them were dying, and many of them would have died if it weren't for Mother Teresa.

It is said that Mother Teresa wanted to go into the center of the besieged city that was currently under bombardment and rescue each one of those children one by one. She was warned by many that it was a mission that could only end in her death, but as she sat in front of those men that warned her, she insisted that there would be a ceasefire soon and they would be able to safely make their way to the children.

It is said that she brokered the ceasefire through prayer and hope. Either way, the bombardment stopped, and Mother Teresa made her way to the front-line hospital to rescue the children. She was accompanied by Red Cross workers as they traveled through the war zone.

The children, all mentally or physically disabled, had been abandoned in the hospital by the staff as they fled the gunfire and bombing. Mother Teresa walked without fear or worry for herself, and one by one, she pulled 37 children from that hospital and rescued them.

Visiting Chernobyl Evacuees

After the nuclear disaster that happened in Chernobyl, thousands of souls were left homeless and ill. They were made to leave their homes in the middle of the night. They didn't have time to pack anything or even take their household pets with them. They were evacuees without a home or a place to go.

Mother Teresa arrived in Moscow in 1986 and visited the resettlement site, where some of the 135,000 evacuees and victims of the Chernobyl nuclear reactor incident had been living. At this point, Mother Teresa had already given her time and her care to so many, setting up homes for the homeless, educating the uneducated, feeding the starving, and caring for the unloved.

While in Moscow, she helped where she could. She gave aid to those that needed it and cared for the thousands of people without homes and without care. Mother Teresa was invited by the Soviet Community to the Soviet Union for the Defense of Peace. This was a state-approved organization that sponsored any exchange with peace groups from around the world.

Mother Teresa accepted the invite with grace and visited the Soviet Union during her time in Moscow.

The Chernobyl disaster was a tragic incident of human error that many to this day still remember and suffer from. Mother Teresa was brave and selfless to help the victims of this incident through their hard, ill, and lonely times. This was another example of how she constantly put her own life at risk in order to better others.

Meeting an Angel

Many speak of the first time they met Mother Teresa. It seemed as though they were meeting someone who was not quite of this world. They said she was like an angel in disguise. It seemed almost unreal to encounter her in person after hearing of her amazing deeds.

In 1995, Father Samuel Martin met Mother Teresa at one of her convents in Rome when he was invited to join the Missionaries of Charity during an early mass. He said that his first impression of her was her remarkable vigor and the attention she paid to others. He noticed her diminutive stature. She was a woman who was alive and fully captivated by her joy and charity. She invited 10 of them to have breakfast with her in a quiet room. He was amazed by the offer. She shared stories with them, and Father Martin explained how it was clear she was a woman that was holy in a way he had never experienced before. She was an undeniable saint of God, and he stated it was unlikely he would ever forget meeting a person like her.

A Teacher and a Saint

"We ourselves feel that what we are doing is just a drop in the ocean. But the ocean would be less because of that missing drop."

- Mother Teresa

Mother Teresa lived a full life, but not the way that others would have lived their life to the fullest. She gave her life entirely to the servitude of others. She wanted to help those that needed it. All she saw was suffering, and she saw the will and power within herself to stop it. She was a religious leader who led others out of poverty and led some on a path of selflessness. She had many lessons to teach the world, and teach them she did.

Don't Do It Because It's Easy

Nothing about anything that Mother Teresa did was easy. Her life and the missions that she chose to undertake were difficult, life-threatening, and sometimes impossible to complete. She did not take on any easy tasks, and she did not turn down something for simply being too hard.

Doing things because they are easy is a quick way to lose faith in yourself and to have your followers lose faith in you. Do not do it because it is easy; do it because you have to.

Sometimes the task ahead of you seems impossible. It seems as though you are bound to fail, so you see no sense in trying. This kind of thinking leads to poor leadership. Greatness comes from seeing what needs to be done and doing it, no matter the difficulty and no matter the cost.

By the end of Mother Teresa's life, she was an old and weak woman. She traveled a lot and risked her own health in order to do what she knew she needed to. She did not take the easy road, and it ended up giving her poor health in the end. She did not regret any of her decisions to do what she did, because she needed to do it.

Push yourself to your limits, and you'll find you can accomplish anything you need to, as long as you know that it is something that needs to be done.

Work With Love

Mother Teresa took great pride in the fact that everything she accomplished she did by acting with love. She did not judge others, hate them, scold them for their past actions, or think that they were responsible for the lives that they were living. She only helped them when they needed her help.

She acted purely out of love, and she put all of her love into every one of her missions. She believed that you could easily help someone through the toughest of times by simply loving them. She was famous for loving the unlovable.

Mother Teresa's motives for spreading love were purely religious. She believed in loving her neighbor as she would love herself, serving her neighbor without throwing stones or passing judgment, and loving her neighbor as if he were Jesus. She felt she was just acting as her religious teachings had told her to. However, there is no reason that the way Mother Teresa treated each of her missions could not be adapted to the life of a great leader.

Working with love is an easy way to make sure that everything you work on is great. Putting love into your work is the same as having passion. You cannot truly be successful if you do not love what you are doing. Leading those who choose to follow you without judgment and treating them only with love can build trust, respect, and mutual affection.

One Person Is Enough of a Difference

If anything, Mother Teresa has taught us that it may take a village to raise a child, but one person is enough to make a difference. She is most famous for her creation of the Missionaries of Charity, in which other sisters and brothers joined her in spreading love and helping others. However, most of her early work was done alone and with no help at all.

Mother Teresa was able to make a difference on a large scale, both as part of an organization and alone. She thought of herself as simply a drop of water in the ocean, as most people often do, but she also realized that a drop of water in the ocean still adds to its rise.

She taught people that they could make a difference, no matter how small and insignificant they think they are.

Suffering for a Greater Cause

It would have been easier for Mother Teresa to stay at home and focus on herself and her own needs. She would have lived a healthy and perhaps a longer life if she didn't care for others and only focused on herself. However, she couldn't do that.

Mother Teresa was okay with suffering because she knew it was for a greater cause. Sacrificing her well-being and life for a cause that was greater than herself seemed worth it.

There is something that any great leader can learn from this. Although you don't have to put your health and life at risk in order to see through an important project or goal, you need to realize that sacrifice and suffering is something you'll have to put up with. Sometimes a leader must take one for the team in order to ensure success. Expecting others to suffer for your cause is the sign of a poor leader, but suffering yourself because you know it's necessary for a greater cause is the sign of true greatness.

Be Generous

Giving was a part of Mother Teresa's nature. She gave emotionally, financially, spiritually, and physically to those who needed it. It might seem like an unnecessary sacrifice, but she said that she found her greatest satisfaction in it. Giving was within her nature, and it made her not only a better person, but a better leader.

You should try being more generous. Although you don't have to give everything that you have to others, you should try to give more. Be more generous when helping those that follow you. Give others more of your time and attention.

When you turn your focus outward onto others and stop looking within, you free yourself of many thoughts and things that can hold you back. When you're a leader, you can't just think of yourself and what is best for you. You need to think of others, especially those that have chosen to follow your leadership. You have to give them everything that they need and, if it comes to it, everything that you have.

9

Bill Gates - The Man Who Led an Entire Generation Into the Future

"We all need people who will give us feedback. That's how we improve."

- Bill Gates

Bill Gates is the co-founder of the Microsoft Corporation, one of the largest and most well-known corporations in the world. He is one of the most prominent leaders in the world today. He was born in 1955 in Washington and has had a life packed full of great achievements and accomplishments.

Building a Company From the Ground Up

Bill Gates' story is not one of rags to riches or from nothing to something. He was born into a family with a fairly wealthy background. His mother was a humble school teacher, but she ended up becoming one of the members of the First Interstate Bank Board of Directors. His father, on the other hand, was a prosperous attorney with a large and wealthy client base. However, even with his privileged childhood, he still found himself working hard in order to get where he is today.

Bill Gates was a brilliant student. He performed exceptionally in all academic subjects, but he especially excelled in mathematics. He developed a passion for programming and computers at the young age of 13 and got himself enrolled in a private preparatory school at the same age. While at school, Bill Gates had a flair for programming, and the Lakeside School noticed this. The school administration made the decision to buy him a computer. His computer came from the General Electric Company, and the school administration allowed him to further pursue any interest he had in computers, including excusing him from his classes. Bill Gates built his very first computer program using this computer he was gifted.

Bill Gates worked with Paul Allen while at school on a system that belonged to Computer Center Corporation.

They worked together to find bugs in the system. Together, along with two other students, they wrote a payroll program for Information Sciences. They did this in order to exchange computer time and royalties. Once they did this, the school became fully aware of the talent that Bill Gates had.

Bill Gates, while working with Paul Allen, worked at a young age to build software, make a name for himself, and start his journey into the world of computers. At the age of 15, he developed and sold software to optimize traffic for around $20,000. A few years later, the same software earned him $30,000, and this is how he started on his journey to becoming one of the world's most successful billionaires.

The Microsoft Corporation is Bill Gates' greatest achievement and the thing that made him famous around the world. He continued to work with Paul Allen even after they left school, and in 1975, they co-founded a software company that was originally named Micro-Soft. While in the initial startup stage, they were unable to hire a sales manager and so the company was delivering small software products to different firms. Bill Gates' mother, Mary Maxwell, helped them with this process.

Very soon into their initial startup, the company started suffering from a financial crisis. This made Gates and Allen realize that their company had dropped to the lowest affordable point. They found that the issue was occurring mainly due to some pirated software they were using. However, struggling is a part of the story, as Gates always believed, and they did not let this development scare them away from what they wanted to build. They both worked to come up with MS-BASIC, which made them a profit of $50,000 at launch and helped to keep their company afloat for a while longer.

Microsoft was offered an opportunity to develop a program by the American multinational tech company IBM. IBM was about to launch the world's first personal computer, but at the time, Microsoft didn't have the resources that they needed in order to develop the operating software for this project. They had to recommend another company to IBM for this operating software since they were unable to help.

Bill Gates always came back fighting from a downfall. Losing the opportunity to be involved in the creation of the world's first personal computer was a big downfall, but he took it in stride. A few months later, Microsoft bought 86-DOS, an operating system, and they started to enhance it. They did this regularly, and on a wide scale, which eventually resulted in the launch of 'MS-DOS.' This was a successful operating system, and it came just before IBM was preparing to launch their personal computer. After the launch of their operating system, Microsoft directly contacted IBM and offered for them to use MS-DOS as the key operating system for their personal computer. IBM accepted their offer instantly, and Microsoft was able to outdo the competition, Digital Research, which was the company IBM originally considered to provide their computer's operating system.

In 1980, Microsoft and IBM signed a contract, and within a year, Microsoft became the Microsoft Corporation. The first ever personal computer the world had ever seen was launched by IBM with MS-DOS and other Microsoft products that Allen Paul and Bill Gates developed, including MS-COBOL, MS-BASIC, MS-PASCAL, and more.

This small company that Paul and Gates founded began collecting accomplishments. Microsoft is credited with the creation of the first mouse for a personal computer and for the development of the Windows Operating System, which is the operating system used by almost everyone in the world today.

The very first Windows Operating System that Microsoft launched was Windows NT. Over the next few years, a series of Windows followed, with each one better, faster, and more capable than the last. This included the launch of Windows 98, Windows 95, Windows 2000, Windows Vista, and Windows XP. Microsoft began growing, and ever since then, it has expanded its available products from the Windows Operating System to several other software. The Microsoft Office Suites, Bing, Office 365, and Hotmail are a few of the software the company has under its belt, but the list keeps going on.

Bill Gates and Paul Allen started at the bottom and built a company from the ground up. They had setbacks that would have caused anyone else to give up or question if they would ever find success. Bill Gates never questioned where he and Allen were going. He knew that they would find their way into the world of computers, and they did. Their company became one of the most powerful names in the modern world when it comes to computers.

Everything began with an idea. Microsoft found its footing slowly, and once it did, it began dominating the software market and kept on going. Today, Bill Gates is one of the most successful individuals in the world, and he still continues to keep up with the pace of an ever-changing world dependent on technology. Microsoft has remained the top software company in the world ever since it first started rising up the ranks.

Microsoft is now a self-running company that needs little involvement from Bill Gates for its day-to-day operations. Most of his time is now spent dedicated to community projects and philanthropy. He has also co-founded several foundations, including The Giving Pledge, a foundation that is meant to focus on encouraging the wealthy community to contribute their wealth toward philanthropic causes.

Bill Gates is known as a powerful and successful man, but he is also known as a giving man. He often funds charities, and upon his death, it's said that over 80 percent of his wealth will be given to multiple charities. Charities he has founded include the Bill and Melinda Gates Foundation and The William H. Gates Foundation.

He continues to be an inspiration to anyone who is looking to create something. He built his world around him and created a worldwide company with just him and one school friend. His life has been an inspiration for many and continues to inspire people around the world to go out there and make something.

A Creator and a Leader of the New World

Bill Gates touched many lives throughout his journey, leaving behind some great stories and inspirational tales for everyone to tell. When anyone talks about him, they talk about his generosity and his willingness to teach others the things he has learned.

A Generous Family

Bill Gates isn't only known for the large company he built and the amazing business skills he possesses. He is also known for his caring nature and his generosity. He came from a wealthy family, and still he worked hard to get to where he was. In a sense, he had nothing because he hadn't earned anything himself, and he wanted to change that. Once he did, he started working towards changing the world.

Bill Gates has started and managed many foundations, all of them working towards bettering the lives of others. One foundation that people just can't seem to stop talking about is the one he started with his wife: the Bill and Melinda Gates Foundation.

The foundation was originally a merger between two already established foundations that Bill Gates created: the William H. Gates Foundation and the Gates Learning Foundation.

The Bill and Melinda Gates Foundation was founded by Melinda French Gates and Bill Gates. It was first launched in the year 2000, and it is now the second-largest charitable foundation in the world.

This is not the only charitable foundation run by Bill Gates, but it is by far the most successful and well known. Its primary goals are to reduce extreme poverty globally, enhance healthcare all around the world while making it more easily available, and expand educational opportunities and access to information technology within the United States.

The reason it is one of the leading charitable industries in the world is because of the way Bill Gates runs it. He manages to apply business techniques to the art of giving, making it successful and helpful at the same time.

Since the creation of their foundation, Bill Gates and his wife have supported and endowed other social, education, and health developments, including establishing the Gates Cambridge Scholarships. These scholarships allow talented and deserving young students the opportunity to study at Cambridge University even if they don't have the means to.

Piracy and the Poor

It's not a secret that many people tend to pirate things that they can't afford to buy, such as movies, music, and games. One program that has a large piracy rate is the Windows Operating System. Bill Gates developed and owns all the different versions of the Windows Operating System, and he is also well aware of how many people are pirating each of the different versions. However, when asked about it in an interview, he made it clear that stopping people from pirating his operating system was not even on his mind.

Bill Gates stated that Microsoft has knowledge of the machines that are using the Windows Operating System, and that includes any machines that are currently running on a pirated version. Because of this, if the pirated version ever connected to the internet, they would be able to stop that pirated operating system from being able to work over the internet; and yet they don't do it.

Most of the pirated versions of the Windows Operating System come from Asian, Indian, and African countries.

Gates knows that some people in these countries aren't able to pay for the operating system, and he would rather they have any version of it at all than no version. They can't afford the service, and their respective governments aren't taking steps toward solving that issue.

Bill Gates believes that if they weren't able to keep using the program, they would lag behind in the race for technology. He would rather they pirate the system than live in a divided world. He sees this as a concern for humanity and not a corporate one. It may be illegal, but he does not see it as unethical, further showing his generosity and kind nature.

Dumpster Diver

Paul Allen and Bill Gates used to do some crazy things when they were still in high school. Paul Allen wrote in his new book that they even used to go dumpster diving.

When they were in high school, they used to hone their programming skills by using a DEC minicomputer that was owned by the local company C-Cubed. Since they were still students, they didn't have access to the amount of information that the company's employees did. This frustrated them as they thought they were falling behind and unable to catch up in the race for information.

One day, the two of them snuck through the shadows at night around the outside of the company. Paul Allen boosted Bill Gates up, since he was the smaller of the two, and onto the top of the company's dumpsters. Bill Gates would look around inside the dumpster for any information that the company had thrown out that they could still use.

He said that they once found a printout of the TOPS-10 source code. With it they were unable to unlock a lot of secrets and keep up with the company's coding skills.

Young Hackers

While in high school, Paul Allen and Bill Gates had to pay for the time they used on the computers. As their charges mounted up, they began looking for different ways they could use the computers without having to pay for their time. Once they decided this, they began looking for different ways they could access one of the free accounts at C-Cube and use it.

It's unclear how they got access to an administrator password, but they did, and they used it to steal one of the company's internal accounting files. Paul Allen and Bill Gates have never gone into detail about how they got the password, but that's how they were able to hack into the company's computers.

They had hoped to decrypt the file and use the information inside to get access to one of their free accounts. However, they were caught by the company and booted out before they could get any information.

Work Hard, Play Hard

Bill Gates would often stay up working hard for days and nights on end. According to Paul Allen, while they were in high school, he would often stay up all night long, working hard until he got the job done.

He continued the habit even after leaving school. One day, a new secretary walked into his office one morning and found Bill Gates sprawled out on the floor. He had been working all night and had fallen asleep on the floor. She thought that he was unconscious and panicked, but he had just been working all weekend and said that was his quick catnap.

Aside from working hard, according to Paul Allen, he also played hard. When their company first started gaining some success, Allen threw a Halloween party at his house. Bill Gates was the life of the party.

He would take a running start at the top of the stairs, and after running as fast as he could, he would throw himself on the banister, belly first. He slid down the banister and glided straight into the kitchen. Paul Allen recounted the story in his new book, explaining how much of a party animal Bill Gates could be.

Plane Hijacking

Bill Gates once hijacked a plane in the early 1980s. He and Paul Allen were late catching a plane at the San Francisco International Airport. The plane pulled away from the jetway, and they missed their flight. Bill Gates and Paul Allen have never stated how important it was for them to catch that plane.

Bill Gates ran up to the control panel that was next to the jetway and started randomly pushing buttons, or at least it would look random to anyone else. He was hoping he would move the jetway back out to the plane. He wanted to hijack the plane and bring it back to the airport to pick them up.

He did not manage to do what he wanted to, but somebody from the airline realized what he was trying to do and called the plane back for them. Paul Allen stated that he was surprised Bill Gates wasn't arrested.

Lessons for Success

"Success is a lousy teacher. It seduces smart people into thinking they can't lose."

- Bill Gates

Bill Gates is one of the wealthiest men in the world, the leader of a new generation, and a great man. He learned many lessons on his way to the place he is today, and he is eager to teach those lessons to others who also wish to seek a greater understanding of leadership and success.

Start Early to End Strong

Bill Gates started as early as he possibly could. He never waited until tomorrow. Everything that he needed to do or wanted to do, he did it straight away. Bill Gates started as early as 13 years old when he started with his work on computers. He states that if you start something as early as possible, that thing will be molded around you.

Starting sooner also means becoming successful earlier as well. You'll also be more willing to continue on your path and not give up. Starting later means finishing later and being more likely to give up if things don't go your way straight away.

Starting early is only half of it. You must also end strong. Bill Gates continued to build his company, growing and growing until he had one of the largest companies and was one of the richest men in the world. He waited until the last final moment to end his journey. Now he is able to rest, allowing his company to run in his absence as he becomes wealthier every day.

You're Weak Alone

Bill Gates never worked alone because he realized at a young age that being alone makes you weak. He built partnerships at every given opportunity. Bill Gates would often form partnerships with people who were more powerful than him: the top dogs. These were people who would call him their 'sidekick.' He was happy with this because he knew that all of these partnerships offered him opportunities to grow and become stronger.

He learned a lot from his partnerships, and soon, he outgrew those who were once above him. Partnerships with others are about learning new skills, taking on new opportunities, and building strong relationships.

Going at it alone makes you weaker than those that are working with partners, and it puts you last in the race. It's better to partner with those that have knowledge to share with you and can help you along your journey than to go it alone.

Life Teaches You the Best Lessons

Bill Gates learned from a young age that although he learned a lot from his schools and his universities, the lessons his teachers taught him were nothing compared to the lessons he learned after he left them.

Bill Gates holds experience higher than learning. Living his life and doing the work taught him more than books and tests could. Experience is the key to being successful in anything.

Real life gives you a real lesson, and it is the hardest lesson you will ever have to learn. So, Bill Gates cautions anyone who wants success in life not to seek the answers to their questions in books but to seek it out in the real world. You'll learn the lesson faster by experiencing it.

Share the Success You Have With Others

Bill Gates is generous not just with his wealth or his knowledge but also with his success. He understands how difficult it is to start your own business and to grow something from nothing. He is always eager to help others reach the same success he has found.

He has stated that a truly successful man is always willing to share that success with others. Knowing the struggles they're going through should compel you to make that struggle a little easier for them.

As a leader, you should always be willing to share your success with others. It builds relationships and helps you grow along with them.

There Are No Shortcuts

There is no way to fast-forward yourself to success. There are no shortcuts and no cheat codes. You must take your journey the slow way. Nothing comes easily, and everything must be worked for. This includes success and greatness.

Bill Gates and Paul Allen started their work at Microsoft a long time ago and on a shaky foundation. They had patience and hard work on their side. With these tools, they were able to surpass many who had started before them, but it was not through the use of shortcuts or easy routes as some believe.

It takes time to build an empire, and it takes a lifetime of consistency to make that empire great. Remember this as you take your journey. Be patient and know that the long road to success is the best one to take.

Conclusion

How would you describe a strong leader? There are many studies that try to find the leadership qualities that take a leader and make them great. There are different kinds of leaders, each one with their own qualities. Each style of leadership requires a different approach. This is why it's difficult to define a truly great leader.

In order to bypass this difficulty, you need to focus on the great part more than the leader part. This book was made not to help you find the qualities that make you a great leader but rather to help you find the qualities of greatness.

What did all of these leaders have in common? It wasn't their leadership style. Abraham Lincoln led with kindness and compassion while showing the ability to compromise and do what needed to be done. Nelson Mandela led with a heart filled with kindness but showed no remorse or resolve when it came to the cause he was fighting for. Mahatma Gandhi sent only love out into the world, taking the route of a pacifist and choosing to lead people with his kind words and bold actions. Mother Teresa used her faith in God and the knowledge that all good things come to those who ask for it to guide her in her journey, helping people along the way if they ask for it or if they need it.

Every single leader mentioned in this book had very few similar qualities, and the way they led the world was completely different. They had to go through completely different things. Nelson Mandela had to lead his world through an unjust rule by an unworthy government. Abraham Lincoln needed to lead a divided nation through a civil war, bringing them together and keeping his country intact. Stephen Hawking desired knowledge, and he needed to lead the world out of darkness and into the next stage of science and human evolution.

Each leader had only one thing in common: they each strived for greatness. Each of them was dealt a set of cards when they were born, and each one of them disagreed with those cards. They did not agree with the life that the world had chosen for them, and they knew they were destined for something greater.

Great leaders are not made by society. Great leaders and great people make themselves. You cannot hope for someone to give you the greatness you seek, and you cannot hope to receive it simply as a birthright. Someone can't be born into greatness, but they can be taught if they are willing to learn.

A promise was made, and a promise was delivered on. You now have the tools you need to seek out greatness for yourself. All you need now is the drive and the willingness to strive for more and realize that you don't have to settle for what others say you are destined for. There is always more out there for those who want it enough.

Take these lessons from the great leaders throughout history that have led the world through the hardest of times and into a new future. Let these lessons be your guide on your journey, and let their words inspire you to want to be more, do more, teach more, learn more, and become more than you are.

Never stop learning and never stop striving for greatness.

"Leadership and learning are indispensable to each other."
- John F. Kennedy

References

Agathangelou, F. (2015). *How to Identify Your Good Qualities When You Feel Worthless | HealthyPlace.* HealthyPlace. https://www.healthyplace.com/blogs/buildingselfesteem/2015/10/identifying-your-good-qualities-when-you-believe-youre-worthless

Alarie, S. *7 Life Lessons from Mother Teresa to Make You a Better Christian.* Finding God Among Us. https://findinggodamongus.com/lessons-from-mother-teresa/

Andrews, E. (2018). *9 Things You May Not Know About Albert Einstein.* History. https://www.history.com/news/9-things-you-may-not-know-about-albert-einstein

Business Connect. (2021). *Success Story of Bill Gates – A Life Filled with Successes.* https://businessconnectindia.in/bill-gates-success-story/

Encyclopedia Britannica. (2022). *Stephen Hawking | Facts, Biography, Books, & Theories.* https://www.britannica.com/biography/Stephen-Hawking

Gur, T. *Never Give In - Lessons From Winston Churchill's Story.* Elevate Abundance. https://elevateabundance.com/winston-churchills-story/

History. (2019). *Mahatma Gandhi.* https://www.history.com/topics/india/mahatma-gandhi

Inspirational Stories. *Motivational Story of Abraham Lincoln, Famous Quotes And Sayings.* https://www.inspirationalstories.com/abraham-lincoln-quotes/

Inspiring Leadership Now. (2020). *Discover 10 Of The Most Inspiring Leaders Of All Time.* https://www.inspiringleadershipnow.com/most-inspiring-leaders-redefine-leadership/

James, R. (2022). *17 Success Lessons from Bill Gates.* Wealthy Gorilla. https://wealthygorilla.com/bill-gates-success-lessons/

Joshi, U. S. *Inspiring Stories from Gandhi's Life.* Bombay Sarvodaya Mandal. https://www.mkgandhi.org/students/story.htm

Kaku, M. (2022). *Albert Einstein | Biography, Education, Discoveries, & Facts.* Encyclopedia Britannica. https://www.britannica.com/biography/Albert-Einstein

Kelly, B. C. (2008). *Best Little Stories from the Life and Times of Winston Churchill.* Cumberland House.

Kosloki, P. (2016). *6 inspiring stories from people who met Mother Teresa.* Aleteia. https://aleteia.org/2016/09/02/6-inspiring-stories-from-people-who-met-mother-teresa/

Leverage Edu. (2021). *15 Great Leaders of the World and their Inspiring Journey.* https://leverageedu.com/blog/great-leaders-of-the-world/

Little, B. (2019). *7 Things You Didn't Know About Stephen Hawking*. History. https://www.history.com/news/7-things-you-didnt-know-about-stephen-hawking

makemegenius. (2021). *Mother Teresa – Inspiring Story of the Self-less Saint Teresa of Kolkata #Mother_Teresa_for_kids* [Video]. YouTube. https://www.youtube.com/watch?v=vuSiOAWlwYM

McKay, B., & McKay, K. (2021). *Lessons in Manliness from Winston Churchill*. The Art of Manliness. https://www.artofmanliness.com/character/manly-lessons/lessons-in-manliness-from-winston-churchill/

Meah, A. *Bill Gates Success Story*. Awaken The Greatness Within. https://www.awakenthegreatnesswithin.com/bill-gates-success-story/

Pomerantz, H. (2019). *Life of Einstein*. The New Yorker. https://www.newyorker.com/magazine/2020/01/06/einstein-the-untold-story

Power Living. (2014). *10 Qualities of Greatness Inspired by Nelson Mandela*. http://www.power-living.com/blog/2014/01/26/10-qualities-of-greatness-in-spired-by-nelson-mandela/

Rosoff, M. (2011). *10 Crazy Stories About Bill Gates From Paul Allen's New Book*. Business Insider. https://www.businessinsider.com/10-things-you-didnt-know-about-bill-gates-2011-4?international=true&r=US&IR=T

The Strive. (2021). *Abraham Lincoln Success Story*. https://thestrive.co/abraham-lincoln-success-story/

Verma, S. (2015). *An Inspirational Story: Stephen Hawking*. YourDOST. https://yourdost.com/blog/2015/11/an-inspirational-story-stephen-hawking.html

Made in the USA
Las Vegas, NV
13 July 2023

74690662R00085